FAVORITE BRAND NAME™

Country Italian

pil

Publications International, Ltd.

Favorite Brand Name Recipes at www.fbnr.com

Copyright © 2001 Publications International, Ltd.
All rights reserved. This publication may not be reproduced or quoted in whole or in part by any means whatsoever without written permission from:

Louis Weber, CEO
Publications International, Ltd.
7373 North Cicero Avenue
Lincolnwood, IL 60712

Permission is never granted for commercial purposes.

Favorite Brand Name is a trademark of Publications International, Ltd.

All recipes and photographs that contain specific brand names are copyrighted by those companies and/or associations, unless otherwise specified. All photographs *except* those on pages 25, 47, 99, 129 and 187 copyright © Publications International, Ltd.

Nestlé and Toll House are registered trademarks of Nestlé.

Some of the products listed in this publication may be in limited distribution.

Front cover photography by Chris Cassidy Photography, Inc.

Inset photos of Italy by Ruth Siegel.

Pictured on the front cover *(clockwise from top center):* Polenta Triangles *(page 318),* Shellfish Cioppino *(page 76),* Pepper-Stuffed Artichokes *(page 290)* and Classic Veal Florentine *(page 156).*
Pictured on the jacket flaps: Caponata *(page 16)* and Florentine Cookies *(page 360).*
Pictured on the back cover *(clockwise from top):* Shrimp Scampi *(page 202),* Lasagna Supreme *(page 86),* Primavera Tortellini en Brodo *(page 72)* and Creamy Chicken Primavera *(page 108).*

ISBN-13: 978-1-4127-2283-4
ISBN-10: 1-4127-2283-7

Library of Congress Catalog Card Number: 2005925712

Manufactured in China.

8 7 6 5 4 3 2 1

Microwave Cooking: Microwave ovens vary in wattage. Use the cooking times as guidelines and check for doneness before adding more time.

Preparation/Cooking Times: Preparation times are based on the approximate amount of time required to assemble the recipe before cooking, baking, chilling or serving. These times include preparation steps such as measuring, chopping and mixing. The fact that some preparations and cooking can be done simultaneously is taken into account. Preparation of optional ingredients and serving suggestions is not included.

CONTENTS

APPETIZERS & SALADS

Fast Pesto Focaccia

> 1 can (10 ounces) pizza crust dough
> 2 tablespoons prepared pesto
> 4 sun-dried tomatoes packed in oil, drained

1. Preheat oven to 425°F. Lightly grease 8×8×2-inch pan. Unroll pizza dough; fold in half and pat into pan.

2. Spread pesto evenly over dough. Chop tomatoes or snip with kitchen scissors; sprinkle over pesto. Press tomatoes into dough. Make indentations in dough every 2 inches using wooden spoon handle.

3. Bake 10 to 12 minutes or until golden brown. Cut into squares and serve warm or at room temperature. *makes 16 appetizers*

prep and cook time: 20 minutes

Fast Pesto Focaccia

Marinated Antipasto

1 cup julienne-sliced carrots
1 cup fresh green beans, cut into 2-inch pieces
1 cup fresh brussels sprouts, quartered
1 cup thinly sliced baby yellow squash
½ cup thinly sliced red bell pepper
½ cup thinly sliced yellow bell pepper
1 can (9 ounces) artichoke hearts, drained, quartered
2 cups water
½ cup white wine vinegar
1 tablespoon olive oil
1 teaspoon sugar
2 bay leaves
1 clove garlic
6 sprigs fresh thyme
¼ teaspoon black pepper
½ cup chopped green onions with tops
½ cup minced parsley
Peel of 2 oranges, cut into thin strips

1. Bring 4 cups water to a boil in large saucepan over high heat. Add carrots, beans and brussels sprouts; cover and simmer 1 minute. Add squash and bell peppers; cover and simmer 1 minute or until vegetables are crisp-tender. Remove from heat; drain. Place vegetables and artichoke hearts in heatproof bowl.

2. Combine 2 cups water, vinegar, oil, sugar, bay leaves, garlic, thyme and black pepper in medium saucepan. Bring to a boil over medium heat. Pour over vegetables; mix well. Cool completely. Cover and refrigerate 12 hours or up to 3 days before serving.

3. Before serving, drain vegetables. Discard bay leaves, garlic and thyme. Toss vegetables with onions, parsley and orange peel.   *makes 8 servings*

Marinated Antipasto

Tuscan White Bean Crostini

    2 cans (15 ounces each) cannellini beans, rinsed and drained
    ½ large red bell pepper, finely chopped *or* ⅓ cup finely chopped roasted red
        bell pepper
    ⅓ cup finely chopped onion
    ⅓ cup red wine vinegar
    3 tablespoons chopped fresh parsley
    1 tablespoon olive oil
    2 cloves garlic, minced
    ½ teaspoon dried oregano leaves
    ¼ teaspoon black pepper
   18 French bread slices, about ¼ inch thick

1. Combine beans, bell pepper and onion in large bowl.

2. Whisk together vinegar, parsley, oil, garlic, oregano and black pepper in small bowl. Pour over bean mixture; toss to coat. Cover; refrigerate 2 hours or overnight.

3. Arrange bread slices in single layer on large nonstick baking sheet or broiler pan. Broil, 6 to 8 inches from heat, 30 to 45 seconds or until bread slices are lightly toasted. Remove; cool completely.

4. Top each toasted bread slice with about 3 tablespoons of bean mixture.

makes 6 servings

 Tip

Cannellini beans are also known as Italian white kidney beans. If they are not available in your supermarket, you may substitute Great Northern beans.

Tuscan White Bean Crostini

Oysters Romano

12 oysters, shucked and on the half shell
2 slices bacon, cut into 12 (1-inch) pieces
½ cup Italian-seasoned dry bread crumbs
2 tablespoons butter or margarine, melted
½ teaspoon garlic salt
6 tablespoons grated Romano, Parmesan or provolone cheese
Fresh chives for garnish

Preheat oven to 375°F. Place shells with oysters on baking sheet. Top each oyster with 1 piece bacon. Bake 10 minutes or until bacon is crisp. Meanwhile, combine bread crumbs, butter and garlic salt in small bowl. Spoon mixture over oysters; top with cheese. Bake 5 to 10 minutes or until cheese melts. Garnish with chives, if desired. Serve immediately.

makes 4 appetizer servings

Hidden Valley® Torta

2 packages (8 ounces *each*) cream cheese
1 packet (1 ounce) Hidden Valley® Original Ranch® Dressing Mix
1 jar (6 ounces) marinated artichoke hearts, drained and chopped
⅓ cup roasted red peppers, drained and chopped
3 tablespoons fresh minced parsley

Beat cream cheese and dressing mix together in medium bowl. In a separate bowl, stir together artichokes, peppers and parsley. In a 3-cup bowl lined with plastic wrap, alternate layers of cream cheese and vegetable mixtures, beginning and ending with a cheese layer.

Chill 4 hours or overnight. Invert on plate; remove plastic wrap. Serve with crackers.

makes 10 to 12 servings

Oysters Romano

Antipasto with Marinated Mushrooms

  Marinated Mushrooms (recipe follows)
4 teaspoons red wine vinegar
½ teaspoon dried basil leaves
½ teaspoon dried oregano leaves
  Generous dash black pepper
¼ cup olive oil
4 ounces mozzarella cheese, cut into ½-inch cubes
4 ounces prosciutto or cooked ham, thinly sliced
4 ounces provolone cheese, cut into 2-inch sticks
1 jar (10 ounces) pepperoncini peppers, drained
8 ounces hard salami, thinly sliced
2 jars (6 ounces each) marinated artichoke hearts, drained
1 can (6 ounces) pitted ripe olives, drained

Prepare Marinated Mushrooms; set aside. Combine vinegar, basil, oregano and black pepper in small bowl. Whisk in oil. Add mozzarella cubes; stir to coat. Marinate, covered, in refrigerator at least 2 hours.

Drain mozzarella cubes; reserve marinade. Wrap ½ of prosciutto slices around provolone sticks; roll up remaining slices separately. Arrange mozzarella cubes, prosciutto-wrapped provolone sticks, prosciutto rolls, Marinated Mushrooms, pepperoncini, salami, artichoke hearts and olives on large platter lined with lettuce, if desired. Drizzle reserved marinade over pepperoncini, artichoke hearts and olives. *makes 6 to 8 servings*

Marinated Mushrooms

½ cup olive oil
3 tablespoons lemon juice
2 tablespoons chopped fresh parsley
½ teaspoon salt
¼ teaspoon dried tarragon leaves
1 clove garlic, slightly crushed
⅛ teaspoon black pepper
½ pound small or medium fresh mushrooms, stems removed

Combine all ingredients except mushrooms in bowl; whisk. Add mushrooms; stir. Chill, covered, at least 4 hours. Drain mushrooms; reserve marinade for dressing, if desired.

Wisconsin Asiago Cheese Puffs

1 cup water
1 tablespoon butter
1 tablespoon olive oil
½ teaspoon salt
  Cayenne pepper to taste
1 cup flour
4 eggs*
½ cup (2 ounces) finely shredded Wisconsin Asiago cheese
½ cup (2 ounces) grated Wisconsin Parmesan cheese

*For lighter puffs, use 2 whole eggs and 4 egg whites.

Preheat oven to 400°F. In small saucepan, combine water, butter, oil, salt and cayenne pepper; bring to a boil. Add flour all at once; stir until mixture forms a smooth ball. Cook over low heat until mixture is drier but still smooth. Put mixture into mixing bowl; beat in eggs, one at a time. Stir in cheeses. Drop spoonfuls of batter onto greased cookie sheet. Bake for 20 minutes or until slightly browned and firm. Serve immediately.   *makes 30 puffs*

Favorite recipe from **Wisconsin Milk Marketing Board**

Tip

Asiago cheese is a semi-firm yellow Italian cheese with a nutty flavor. It is available in small wheels and blocks.

Venetian Canapés

12 slices firm white bread
 5 tablespoons butter or margarine, divided
 2 tablespoons all-purpose flour
½ cup milk
 3 ounces fresh mushrooms (about 9 medium), finely chopped
 6 tablespoons grated Parmesan cheese, divided
 2 teaspoons anchovy paste
¼ teaspoon salt
⅛ teaspoon black pepper
   Green and ripe olive slices, red and green bell pepper strips and rolled
     anchovy fillets, for garnish

Preheat oven to 350°F. Cut two rounds out of each bread slice with 2-inch round cutter. Melt 3 tablespoons butter in small saucepan. Brush both sides of bread rounds lightly with butter. Bake bread rounds on ungreased baking sheet 5 to 6 minutes per side or until golden. Remove to wire rack. Cool completely. *Increase oven temperature to 425°F.*

Melt remaining 2 tablespoons butter in same small saucepan. Stir in flour; cook and stir over medium heat until bubbly. Whisk in milk; cook and stir 1 minute or until sauce thickens and bubbles. (Sauce will be very thick.) Place mushrooms in large bowl; stir in sauce, 3 tablespoons cheese, anchovy paste, salt and black pepper until well blended.

Spread 1 heaping teaspoon mushroom mixture onto each toast round; place on ungreased baking sheets. Sprinkle remaining 3 tablespoons cheese over bread rounds, dividing evenly. Bake 5 to 7 minutes or until tops are light brown. Serve warm.

makes about 2 dozen appetizers

Venetian Canapés

Caponata

1 medium eggplant (about 1 pound), peeled and cut into ½-inch pieces
1 can (14½ ounces) diced Italian plum tomatoes, undrained
1 medium onion, chopped
1 red bell pepper, cut into ½-inch pieces
½ cup prepared medium-hot salsa
¼ cup extra-virgin olive oil
2 tablespoons capers, drained
2 tablespoons balsamic vinegar
3 cloves garlic, minced
1 teaspoon dried oregano leaves
¼ teaspoon salt
⅓ cup packed fresh basil, cut into thin strips
   Toasted sliced Italian or French bread

Slow Cooker Directions
Mix all ingredients except basil and bread in slow cooker. Cover and cook on LOW 7 to 8 hours or until vegetables are crisp-tender. Stir in basil. Serve at room temperature on toasted bread.   *makes about 5¼ cups*

Crostini

¼ loaf whole wheat baguette (4 ounces)
4 plum tomatoes
1 cup (4 ounces) shredded part-skim mozzarella cheese
3 tablespoons prepared pesto sauce

1. Preheat oven to 400°F. Slice baguette into 16 very thin, diagonal slices. Slice each tomato vertically into four ¼-inch slices.

2. Place baguette slices on nonstick baking sheet. Top each with 1 tablespoon cheese, then 1 slice tomato. Bake 8 minutes or until bread is lightly toasted and cheese is melted. Remove from oven; top each crostini with about ½ teaspoon pesto sauce. Serve warm.

makes 8 servings

Caponata

Tomato-Artichoke Focaccia

1 package (16 ounces) hot roll mix
2 tablespoons wheat bran
1¼ cups hot water
4 teaspoons olive oil, divided
1 cup thinly sliced onions
2 cloves garlic, minced
1 cup rehydrated sun-dried tomatoes (4 ounces dry), cut into strips
1 cup artichoke hearts, sliced
1 tablespoon minced fresh rosemary
2 tablespoons freshly grated Parmesan cheese

1. Preheat oven to 400°F. Combine dry ingredients and yeast packet from hot roll mix in large bowl. Add bran; mix well. Stir in hot water and 2 teaspoons oil. Knead dough about 5 minutes or until ingredients are blended.

2. Spray 15½×11½-inch baking pan or 14-inch pizza pan with nonstick cooking spray. Press dough onto bottom of prepared pan. Cover; let rise 15 minutes.

3. Heat 1 teaspoon oil in medium skillet over low heat. Add onions and garlic; cook and stir 2 to 3 minutes or until onions are tender.

4. Brush surface of dough with remaining teaspoon oil. Top dough with onion mixture, tomatoes, artichokes and fresh rosemary. Sprinkle with Parmesan.

5. Bake 25 to 30 minutes or until lightly browned on top. Cut into squares. Garnish each square with fresh rosemary sprigs, if desired.

makes 16 servings

Tip

To rehydrate sun-dried tomatoes, cover them with hot water for 30 minutes or boiling water for 5 minutes. Drain before using.

Rosemary-Roasted Vegetable Crostini

1 small eggplant (about ¾ pound)
1 medium zucchini
1 medium red onion
1 medium green bell pepper
2 Italian plum tomatoes, seeded
4 medium cloves garlic, minced
¼ cup dry white wine or orange juice
2 tablespoons tarragon white wine vinegar
1 tablespoon olive oil
1 tablespoon chopped fresh rosemary *or* 1 teaspoon dried rosemary, crushed
¼ teaspoon black pepper
1 sourdough bread loaf (1 pound), 12 to 14 inches long
1 cup (4 ounces) shredded part-skim mozzarella cheese

1. Preheat oven to 400°F.

2. Trim ends from eggplant and zucchini; discard. Cut all vegetables into ¼-inch pieces. Place vegetables in large bowl. Add garlic, wine, vinegar, oil and seasonings; toss to coat evenly. Transfer to nonstick 15×10×1-inch jelly-roll pan.

3. Bake 45 minutes or until lightly browned, stirring every 15 minutes.

4. Spray large nonstick baking sheets with nonstick cooking spray. Trim ends from bread; cut into ½-inch-thick slices. Arrange slices in single layer on prepared baking sheets. Bake 3 minutes on each side or until crisp and lightly browned on both sides.

5. Spoon vegetable mixture evenly onto toasted bread slices; sprinkle evenly with cheese. Continue baking 5 minutes or until mixture is heated through and cheese is melted. Transfer to serving plates; garnish, if desired. *makes 12 servings*

Herbed Croutons with Savory Bruschetta

½ cup regular or reduced fat mayonnaise
¼ cup *French's®* Dijon Mustard
1 tablespoon finely chopped green onion
1 clove garlic, minced
¾ teaspoon dried oregano leaves
1 long thin loaf (18 inches) French bread, cut crosswise into ½-inch-thick slices
Savory Bruschetta (recipe follows)

Combine mayonnaise, mustard, onion, garlic and oregano in small bowl; mix well. Spread herbed mixture on one side of each slice of bread.

Place bread, spread sides up, on grid. Grill over medium-low coals 1 minute or until lightly toasted. Spoon Savory Bruschetta onto herbed croutons. Serve warm.

makes 6 appetizer servings

prep time: 10 minutes
cook time: 1 minute

Savory Bruschetta

1 pound ripe plum tomatoes, cored, seeded and chopped
1 cup finely chopped fennel bulb or celery
¼ cup chopped fresh basil leaves
3 tablespoons *French's®* Dijon Mustard
3 tablespoons olive oil
3 tablespoons balsamic vinegar
2 cloves garlic, minced
½ teaspoon salt

Combine ingredients in medium bowl; toss well to coat evenly. *makes 3 cups*

prep time: 15 minutes

Herbed Croutons with Savory Bruschetta

Mediterranean Frittata

¼ cup olive oil
5 small yellow onions, thinly sliced
1 can (14½ ounces) whole peeled tomatoes, drained and chopped
¼ pound prosciutto or cooked ham, chopped
¼ cup grated Parmesan cheese
2 tablespoons chopped fresh parsley
½ teaspoon dried marjoram leaves
¼ teaspoon dried basil leaves
¼ teaspoon salt
Generous dash black pepper
6 eggs
2 tablespoons butter or margarine
Italian parsley leaves for garnish

1. Heat oil in medium skillet over medium-high heat. Cook and stir onions in hot oil 6 to 8 minutes until soft and golden. Add tomatoes. Cook and stir over medium heat 5 minutes. Remove tomatoes and onions to large bowl with slotted spoon; discard drippings. Cool tomato-onion mixture to room temperature.

2. Stir prosciutto, cheese, parsley, marjoram, basil, salt and pepper into cooled tomato-onion mixture. Whisk eggs in small bowl; stir into prosciutto mixture.

3. Preheat broiler. Heat butter in large broilerproof skillet over medium heat until melted and bubbly; reduce heat to low.

4. Add egg mixture to skillet, spreading evenly. Cook over low heat 8 to 10 minutes until all but top ¼ inch of egg mixture is set; shake pan gently to test. *Do not stir.*

5. Broil egg mixture about 4 inches from heat 1 to 2 minutes until top of egg mixture is set. (Do not brown or frittata will be dry.) Frittata can be served hot, at room temperature or cold. To serve, cut into wedges. Garnish, if desired.   *makes 6 to 8 appetizer servings*

Mediterranean Frittata

Roasted Red Pepper Pesto Cheesecake

1 cup butter-flavored cracker crumbs (about 40 crackers)
¼ cup (½ stick) butter *or* margarine, melted
2 packages (8 ounces each) PHILADELPHIA® Cream Cheese, softened
1 cup ricotta cheese
3 eggs
½ cup KRAFT® 100% Grated Parmesan Cheese
½ cup DI GIORNO® Pesto
½ cup drained roasted red peppers, puréed

MIX crumbs and butter. Press onto bottom of 9-inch springform pan. Bake at 325°F for 10 minutes.

MIX cream cheese and ricotta cheese with electric mixer on medium speed until well blended. Add eggs, 1 at a time, mixing well after each addition. Blend in remaining ingredients. Pour over crust.

BAKE at 325°F for 55 minutes to 1 hour or until center is almost set. Run knife or metal spatula around rim of pan to loosen cake; cool before removing rim of pan. Refrigerate 4 hours or overnight. Let stand at room temperature 15 minutes before serving. Store leftover cheesecake in refrigerator.   *makes 12 to 14 servings*

prep: 15 minutes plus refrigerating
bake: 1 hour plus standing

Tip

Pesto is an uncooked sauce made from fresh basil leaves, garlic, pine nuts, Parmesan cheese and olive oil. Look for it in the refrigerated case of the supermarket with the fresh pastas.

Roasted Red Pepper Pesto Cheesecake

Italian-Style Stuffed Mushrooms

2 pounds large mushrooms (about 2 inches each)
½ cup (1 stick) I CAN'T BELIEVE IT'S NOT BUTTER!® Spread
⅓ cup chopped onion
1 tablespoon chopped garlic
1 cup Italian seasoned dry bread crumbs
⅔ cup shredded mozzarella cheese (about 2½ ounces)
¼ cup grated Parmesan cheese
2 tablespoons chopped fresh parsley
1 tablespoon red wine vinegar
⅛ teaspoon ground black pepper
¼ teaspoon salt

Preheat oven to 400°F.

Remove and chop mushroom stems.

In 12-inch skillet, melt I Can't Believe It's Not Butter! Spread over medium-high heat and cook mushroom stems and onion, stirring occasionally, 5 minutes or until tender.

Add garlic and cook 30 seconds. In medium bowl, pour mushroom mixture over bread crumbs. Stir in cheeses, parsley, vinegar and pepper.

Sprinkle mushroom caps with salt. On baking sheet, arrange mushroom caps; evenly spoon mushroom mixture into mushroom caps.

Bake 25 minutes or until mushrooms are tender and golden.   *makes about 20 mushrooms*

Bruschetta

　　1 cup thinly sliced onion
　　½ cup chopped seeded tomato
　　2 tablespoons capers
　　¼ teaspoon black pepper
　　3 cloves garlic, finely chopped
　　1 teaspoon olive oil
　　4 slices French bread
　　½ cup (2 ounces) shredded reduced-fat Monterey Jack cheese

1. Spray large nonstick skillet with nonstick cooking spray. Heat over medium heat until hot. Add onion. Cook and stir 5 minutes. Stir in tomato, capers and pepper. Cook 3 minutes.

2. Preheat broiler. Combine garlic and oil in small bowl; brush bread slices with mixture. Top with onion mixture; sprinkle with cheese. Place on baking sheet. Broil 3 minutes or until cheese melts. *makes 4 servings*

Toasted Pesto Rounds

　　¼ cup thinly sliced fresh basil or chopped fresh dill
　　¼ cup (1 ounce) grated Parmesan cheese
　　1 medium clove garlic, minced
　　3 tablespoons reduced-calorie mayonnaise
　12 French bread slices, about ¼ inch thick
　　4 teaspoons chopped tomato
　　1 green onion with top, sliced
　　　Black pepper

1. Preheat broiler.

2. Combine basil, cheese, garlic and mayonnaise in small bowl; mix well.

3. Arrange bread slices in single layer on large nonstick baking sheet or broiler pan. Broil, 6 to 8 inches from heat, 30 to 45 seconds or until bread slices are lightly toasted.

4. Turn bread slices over; spread evenly with basil mixture. Broil 1 minute or until lightly browned. Top evenly with tomato and green onion. Season to taste with pepper. Transfer to serving plate. *makes 12 servings*

Rotini Salad

 10 ounces rotini pasta
 2 to 3 stalks broccoli
 1 can (6 ounces) small pitted ripe olives, drained
 10 to 12 cherry tomatoes, cut into halves
 ½ medium red onion, cut into slivers
 ½ cup Italian salad dressing
 1 to 2 tablespoons grated Parmesan cheese (optional)
 Black pepper
 Carrot strips for garnish

1. Cook pasta according to package directions. Drain in colander. Cover and refrigerate until chilled.

2. Trim leaves from broccoli stalks. Trim ends of stalks. Cut broccoli into flowerets by removing each head to include a small piece of the stem. Peel stalks, then cut into 1-inch pieces.

3. To cook broccoli, bring 1 quart lightly salted water to a boil in 2-quart saucepan over high heat. Immediately add broccoli; return to a boil. Continue boiling, uncovered, 3 to 5 minutes until bright green and tender. Drain broccoli; rinse under cold water and drain thoroughly.

4. Combine pasta, broccoli, olives, tomatoes, onion and salad dressing in large bowl. Add cheese. Season to taste with pepper. Toss gently to coat.

5. Cover; refrigerate at least 2 hours. Garnish, if desired.   *makes 8 to 10 servings*

Rotini Salad

Marinated Vegetable Salad

3 tablespoons plus 1½ teaspoons white wine vinegar
2 tablespoons minced fresh basil *or* ½ teaspoon dried basil leaves
½ teaspoon salt
⅛ teaspoon black pepper
  Dash sugar
6 tablespoons olive oil
2 ripe medium tomatoes
⅓ cup pitted green olives
⅓ cup Italian- or Greek-style black olives
1 head leaf or red leaf lettuce
1 small head curly endive
2 heads Belgian endive

1. For dressing, place vinegar, basil, salt, pepper and sugar in food processor or blender. With motor running, add oil in slow steady stream until oil is thoroughly blended.

2. Cut tomatoes into wedges. Combine tomatoes and green and black olives in medium bowl. Add dressing; toss lightly. Cover and let stand at room temperature 30 minutes to blend flavors, stirring occasionally.

3. Rinse leaf lettuce and curly endive; drain well. Refrigerate greens until ready to assemble salad. Core Belgian endive and separate leaves; rinse and drain well.

4. To serve, layer leaf lettuce, curly endive and Belgian endive leaves in large, shallow bowl.

5. Remove tomatoes and olives with slotted spoon and place on top of greens. Spoon remaining dressing over salad. Serve immediately or cover and refrigerate up to 30 minutes.

makes 6 servings

Marinated Vegetable Salad

Italian Crouton Salad

6 ounces French or Italian bread
¼ cup plain nonfat yogurt
¼ cup red wine vinegar
4 teaspoons olive oil
1 tablespoon water
3 cloves garlic, minced
6 medium (about 12 ounces) plum tomatoes
½ medium red onion, thinly sliced
3 tablespoons slivered fresh basil leaves
2 tablespoons finely chopped fresh parsley
12 leaves red leaf lettuce *or* 4 cups prepared Italian salad mix
2 tablespoons grated Parmesan cheese

1. Preheat broiler. Cut bread into ¾-inch cubes. Place in single layer on baking sheet. Broil, 4 inches from heat, 3 minutes or until bread is golden, stirring every 30 seconds to 1 minute. Remove from baking sheet; place in large bowl.

2. Whisk together yogurt, vinegar, oil, water and garlic in small bowl until blended; set aside. Core tomatoes; cut into ¼-inch slices. Add to bread along with onion, basil and parsley; stir until blended. Pour yogurt mixture over crouton mixture; toss to coat. Cover; refrigerate 30 minutes or up to 1 day. (Croutons will be more tender the following day.)

3. To serve, place lettuce on plates. Spoon crouton mixture over lettuce. Sprinkle with Parmesan cheese. *makes 6 servings*

 Tip

To sliver basil leaves, layer leaves with largest leaves on the bottom. Roll up and slice basil into ¼-inch-thick slices. Separate basil into strips.

Italian Crouton Salad

Orzo and Summer Squash Salad

1⅓ cups (8 ounces) uncooked orzo pasta
3 cups diced zucchini and/or yellow summer squash (½-inch pieces)
1 cup diced tomato
½ cup prepared light or regular Caesar salad dressing
1 teaspoon dried basil leaves*
Fresh spinach leaves
Salt and black pepper

You may substitute ¼ cup julienned fresh basil leaves for dried basil leaves.

1. Cook orzo according to package directions adding squash for last 2 minutes of cooking. Drain well; rinse under cold water to stop cooking.

2. Place mixture in large bowl; stir in tomato. Pour dressing over salad; sprinkle with basil. Toss gently to coat. Cover and refrigerate until cool. Serve salad over spinach leaves. Season to taste with salt and pepper.   *makes 6 (1-cup) servings*

serving suggestion: Serve alongside simply grilled poultry, pork or fish.

prep and cook time: 25 minutes

Tip
Orzo is a pasta made in the shape of rice. It is most often used in soups, salads and as a substitute for rice.

Orzo and Summer Squash Salad

Tomato, Mozzarella & Basil Salad

　2 tablespoons red wine vinegar
　1 clove garlic, minced
　½ teaspoon salt
　¼ teaspoon dry mustard
　　Generous dash black pepper
　⅓ cup olive or vegetable oil
　4 Italian plum tomatoes
　6 ounces mozzarella cheese
　8 to 10 fresh basil leaves

1. For dressing, combine vinegar, garlic, salt, mustard and pepper in small bowl. Add oil in slow steady stream, whisking until oil is thoroughly blended.

2. Slice tomatoes and cheese into ¼-inch-thick slices. Trim cheese slices to size of tomato slices.

3. Place tomato and cheese slices in large, shallow bowl or glass baking dish. Pour dressing over slices. Marinate, covered, in refrigerator at least 30 minutes or up to 3 hours, turning slices occasionally.

4. Layer basil leaves with largest leaf on bottom, then roll up jelly-roll fashion. Slice basil roll into ¼-inch-thick slices; separate into strips.

5. Arrange tomato and cheese slices alternately on serving plate or 4 individual salad plates. Sprinkle with basil strips; drizzle with remaining dressing. *makes 4 servings*

Tomato, Mozzarella & Basil Salad

Fennel, Olive and Radicchio Salad

  11 Italian- or Greek-style black olives, divided
  ¼ cup olive oil
   1 tablespoon lemon juice
   1 flat anchovy fillet *or* ½ teaspoon anchovy paste
  ¼ teaspoon salt
     Generous dash black pepper
     Generous dash sugar
   1 fresh fennel bulb
   1 head radicchio*
     Fennel greenery for garnish

Radicchio, a tart red chicory, is available in large supermarkets and specialty food shops. If not available, 2 heads of Belgian endive can be used; although it does not provide the dramatic red color, it will give a similar texture and flavor

1. For dressing, cut 3 olives in half; remove and discard pits. Place pitted olives, oil, lemon juice and anchovy in food processor or blender; process 5 seconds. Add salt, pepper and sugar; process until olives are finely chopped, about 5 seconds more. Set aside.

2. Cut off and discard fennel stalks. Cut off and discard root end at base of fennel bulb and any discolored parts of bulb. Cut fennel bulb lengthwise into 8 wedges; separate each wedge into segments.

3. Separate radicchio leaves; rinse thoroughly under running water. Drain well.

4. Arrange radicchio leaves, fennel and remaining olives on serving plate. Spoon dressing over salad. Garnish, if desired. Serve immediately.   *makes 4 servings*

Tip

Fennel (also called bulb fennel, sweet anise or finocchio) is widely used as a vegetable in Mediterranean cuisines. The bulbous base slightly resembles celery in appearance and texture and stalks are topped by feathery green leaves.

Rice Salad Milano

3 cups hot cooked rice
2 tablespoons vegetable oil
2 tablespoons lemon juice
1 clove garlic, minced
½ teaspoon salt (optional)
½ teaspoon dried rosemary leaves
½ teaspoon dried oregano leaves
½ teaspoon ground black pepper
1 small zucchini, julienned*
1 medium tomato, seeded and chopped
2 tablespoons grated Parmesan cheese

To julienne, slice zucchini diagonally. Cut slices into matchstick-size strips.

Place rice in large bowl. Combine oil, lemon juice, garlic, salt, rosemary, oregano, and pepper in small jar with lid; shake well. Pour over rice; toss lightly. Cover; let cool. Add remaining ingredients. Serve at room temperature or chilled.   *makes 6 servings*

Favorite recipe from **USA Rice Federation**

Italian Vegetable Salad

1 package (9 ounces) DI GIORNO® Three Cheese Tortellini, cooked, drained
1 small zucchini, cut in half lengthwise, sliced
½ each green and red pepper, chopped
½ cup halved cherry tomatoes
½ cup prepared GOOD SEASONS® Reduced Calorie Italian or Zesty Italian
    Salad Dressing
2 green onions, diagonally sliced

TOSS all ingredients in large bowl; cover. Refrigerate at least 2 hours.

STIR in additional dressing just before serving, if desired.   *makes 8 servings*

prep time: 10 minutes plus refrigerating

Quick Vegetable & Pesto Salad

¼ cup reduced-fat mayonnaise
¼ cup refrigerated pesto sauce
1 tablespoon balsamic vinegar
6 cups assorted vegetables from salad bar, such as sliced mushrooms, shredded
    carrots, red onion strips, sliced radishes, peas, broccoli florets and bell
    pepper strips (about 1½ pounds)
Lettuce leaves

1. Combine mayonnaise, pesto and vinegar in large bowl; stir until well blended.

2. Add vegetables; toss well to coat. Cover and refrigerate 10 minutes. Arrange lettuce leaves on salad plates. Top with vegetable mixture. *makes 6 (1-cup) servings*

note: Chilling for 30 minutes will improve the flavor of this easy side-dish salad.

prep time: 15 minutes

Panzanella (Italian Bread Salad)

4 ounces day-old French bread, cubed
4 plum tomatoes, chopped
3 tablespoons extra-virgin olive oil
2 tablespoons red wine vinegar
¼ cup chopped fresh basil
1 clove garlic, minced
½ teaspoon salt

1. Combine bread cubes and tomatoes in medium serving bowl.

2. Whisk together oil, vinegar, basil, garlic and salt in small bowl. Pour over bread mixture; toss until well mixed. *makes 6 servings*

note: You can substitute day-old whole wheat bread, sour dough bread or lightly toasted pita bread for the Italian bread. Simply cube it or tear it into small pieces.

Quick Vegetable & Pesto Salad

SOUPS & STEWS

Quick Tuscan Bean, Tomato and Spinach Soup

2 cans (14½ ounces each) diced tomatoes with onions, undrained
1 can (14½ ounces) fat-free, reduced-sodium chicken broth
2 teaspoons sugar
2 teaspoons dried basil leaves
¾ teaspoon reduced-sodium Worcestershire sauce
1 can (15 ounces) small white beans, rinsed and drained
3 ounces fresh baby spinach leaves or chopped spinach leaves
2 teaspoons extra-virgin olive oil

Combine tomatoes with liquid, chicken broth, sugar, basil and Worcestershire sauce in Dutch oven or large saucepan; bring to a boil over high heat. Reduce heat and simmer, uncovered, 10 minutes.

Stir in beans and spinach and cook 5 minutes longer or until spinach is tender.

Remove from heat; stir in oil just before serving. *makes 4 (1½-cup) servings*

Quick Tuscan Bean, Tomato and
Spinach Soup

Ravioli Soup

8 ounces sweet Italian sausage, casing removed
1 clove garlic, crushed
2 (14¼-ounce) cans lower sodium chicken broth
2 cups water
1 (9-ounce) package frozen miniature cheese-filled ravioli
1 (15-ounce) can garbanzo beans, drained
1 (14½-ounce) can stewed tomatoes
⅓ cup GREY POUPON® Dijon Mustard
½ teaspoon dried oregano leaves
¼ teaspoon coarsely ground black pepper
1 cup torn fresh spinach leaves
    Grated Parmesan cheese

1. Brown sausage and cook garlic in 4-quart heavy pot over medium heat until tender, stirring to break up sausage, about 5 minutes. Pour off excess fat; remove sausage mixture from pot and set aside.

2. Heat chicken broth and water to a boil in same pot over medium-high heat. Add ravioli; cook for 4 to 5 minutes or until tender. Stir in beans, stewed tomatoes, sausage mixture, mustard, oregano and pepper; heat through. Stir in spinach and cook until wilted, about 1 minute. Serve topped with Parmesan cheese.   *makes 8 servings*

Tip

Garbanzo beans, also known as chick-peas or ceci beans, are popular in the cuisines of the Mediterranean region and the Middle East. They are the basic ingredient in hummus and an important ingredient in soups and couscous dishes.

Ravioli Soup

Minute Minestrone with Bays® Crostini

    2 cans (15 ounces each) country vegetable soup
    2 leaves romaine lettuce, chopped
    2 slices prosciutto, chopped (optional)
    ½ medium zucchini, sliced
    2 tablespoons grated Asiago cheese
    1 cup leftover cooked pasta
      Olive oil
    4 teaspoons prepared pesto
      Chopped Italian parsley
      Grated lemon peel
      BAYS® Crostini (recipe follows)

In a large saucepan, combine soup, lettuce, prosciutto, zucchini and cheese. Heat over low heat, stirring occasionally, until hot and bubbly. In a skillet over low heat, toss pasta with oil to heat thoroughly. Ladle soup into individual bowls. Stir one teaspoonful of prepared pesto into each serving. Spoon pasta on top; sprinkle with parsley and lemon peel. Serve with Bays® Crostini. *makes 4 servings*

Other additions: Leftover cooked sugar snap peas or green beans, cut up; pepperoni or chopped ham.

Bays® Crostini

    2 tablespoons olive oil
    1 teaspoon dry Italian salad dressing mix
    4 BAYS® English muffins, split
    2 tablespoons grated Asiago cheese
    1 tablespoon grated Romano cheese

Combine oil and dressing mix; brush on both muffin halves. Place on baking sheet. Bake in a preheated 325°F oven for 15 minutes. Remove from oven; sprinkle with cheeses. Serve warm or at room temperature.

Minute Minestrone with Bays® Crostini

Pasta e Fagioli

1 teaspoon olive oil
3 cloves garlic, minced
1 can (15 ounces) cannellini or Great Northern beans, rinsed and drained
2 cans (about 14 ounces each) fat-free reduced-sodium chicken broth
½ cup white wine, divided
1 tablespoon dried basil leaves
½ teaspoon black pepper
¼ to ½ teaspoon red pepper flakes
6 ounces uncooked ditalini pasta or other small tube pasta
4 teaspoons grated Parmesan cheese

Heat oil in large saucepan over medium-low heat until hot. Add garlic and beans; cook and stir 3 minutes. Add chicken broth, ¼ cup wine, basil, pepper and red pepper flakes. Bring to a boil over medium-high heat. Add pasta; cook 10 to 12 minutes or until tender. Add remaining ¼ cup wine just prior to pasta being fully cooked. Sprinkle with grated cheese. Serve immediately. *makes 4 (1-cup) servings*

note: This soup will be very thick.

Chicken Tortellini Soup

1 can (49½ ounces) chicken broth
1 package PERDUE® SHORT CUTS® Fresh Italian Carved Chicken Breast
1 package (9 ounces) fresh pesto or cheese tortellini or tortelloni
1 cup fresh spinach or arugula leaves, shredded
¼ to ½ cup grated Parmesan cheese

In large saucepan over medium-high heat, bring broth to a boil. Add chicken and tortellini; cook 6 to 8 minutes, until pasta is tender, reducing heat to keep a gentle boil. Just before serving, stir in fresh spinach. Ladle soup into bowls and sprinkle with Parmesan cheese. *makes 4 servings*

prep time: 5 minutes
cook time: 15 minutes

Chicken Cioppino

1 whole fryer (about 3½ pounds), cut into pieces
3 tablespoons olive oil
1 cup chopped onion
1 small red or green bell pepper, diced
4 cloves garlic, minced
1 (28-ounce) can crushed whole tomatoes with liquid
1 (8-ounce) can tomato sauce
1 cup chicken broth
½ cup dry white wine
6 tablespoons minced fresh parsley, divided
6 fresh basil leaves, chopped
6 thin lemon slices
⅛ teaspoon salt
⅛ teaspoon white pepper
1 pound cleaned fresh shrimp
1 pound cooked spaghetti or other pasta

Heat 2 tablespoons olive oil in heavy large skillet over medium-high heat. Add chicken and sauté until golden on all sides, about 3 minutes per side. Remove to platter; drain any chicken fat from skillet.

Reduce heat to medium-low and add remaining 1 tablespoon olive oil, onion, bell pepper and garlic. Sauté for 3 to 4 minutes until soft. Add tomatoes, tomato sauce, broth, wine, 5 tablespoons parsley, basil, lemon slices, salt and white pepper; cover and simmer for 15 minutes to allow flavors to blend.

Add chicken and simmer partially covered for another 30 minutes until chicken is tender. Add shrimp, simmering on low heat for 5 minutes longer. Serve chicken and shrimp with sauce in deep plates over pasta. Garnish each portion with remaining parsley.

makes 4 servings

Favorite recipe from **National Chicken Council**

Classic Meatball Soup

2 pounds beef bones, rinsed
3 ribs celery
2 carrots
1 medium onion, cut in half
1 bay leaf
6 cups cold water
1 egg
4 tablespoons chopped fresh parsley, divided
1 teaspoon salt, divided
½ teaspoon dried marjoram leaves, crushed
¼ teaspoon black pepper, divided
½ cup soft fresh bread crumbs
¼ cup grated Parmesan cheese
1 pound ground beef
1 can (14½ ounces) whole peeled tomatoes, undrained
½ cup uncooked rotini or small macaroni

1. To make stock, combine bones, celery, carrots, onion and bay leaf in 6-quart stockpot. Add water. Bring to a boil. Reduce heat and simmer, partially covered 1 hour, skimming foam occasionally.

2. Meanwhile, preheat oven to 400°F. Spray 13×9-inch baking pan with nonstick cooking spray. Combine egg, 3 tablespoons parsley, ½ teaspoon salt, marjoram and ⅛ teaspoon pepper in medium bowl; whisk lightly. Stir in bread crumbs and cheese. Add beef; mix well. Shape meat mixture into 1-inch meatballs. Place meatballs in prepared pan; bake 20 to 25 minutes until brown and cooked through, turning occasionally. Drain on paper towels.

3. Strain stock through sieve into bowl. Slice celery and carrots; reserve. Discard bones, onion and bay leaf. To degrease stock, let stand 5 minutes to allow fat to rise. Skim off fat.

4. Return stock to stockpot. Drain tomatoes, reserving juice. Chop tomatoes; add to stock with juice. Bring to a boil; boil 5 minutes. Stir in rotini, remaining ½ teaspoon salt and ⅛ teaspoon pepper. Cook 6 minutes, stirring occasionally. Add reserved vegetables and meatballs. Reduce heat to medium; cook 10 minutes until hot. Stir in remaining 1 tablespoon parsley. Season to taste.

makes 4 to 6 servings

Classic Meatball Soup

Tortellini Soup

½ pound mild or hot Italian sausage links
½ cup water
1 tablespoon olive oil
1 medium onion, chopped
2 cloves garlic, minced
4 cups canned beef broth
1 can (16 ounces) whole tomatoes, drained and chopped
1 carrot, sliced
1 teaspoon dried oregano leaves, crushed
1 teaspoon dried basil leaves, crushed
½ teaspoon salt
¼ teaspoon black pepper
1 small zucchini, halved, sliced
1 package (9 ounces) refrigerated, cheese-filled tortellini*
Grated Parmesan cheese

Do not use frozen tortellini.

1. Cook sausage in medium skillet over medium heat 7 minutes or until evenly browned, turning occasionally. Add water. Reduce heat to low. Cover and simmer 20 minutes. Drain; allow sausage to stand at room temperature until cool enough to handle.

2. Heat oil in 5-quart Dutch oven over medium heat. Cook and stir onion and garlic in oil 4 minutes or until onion is soft.

3. Stir in broth, tomatoes, carrot, oregano, basil, salt and pepper. Bring to a boil over high heat. Reduce heat and simmer, uncovered, 30 minutes, stirring occasionally.

4. Cut sausage into thin slices; add to Dutch oven. Simmer 10 minutes.

5. Bring soup to a boil over high heat. Add zucchini and tortellini. Gently boil 7 minutes or until pasta is just tender.

6. Ladle into bowls. Sprinkle each serving with cheese; serve immediately.

makes 6 servings

note: Tortellini continues to absorb liquid while standing. It may be necessary to add additional broth when reheating soup.

Tortellini Soup

Cioppino

1 teaspoon olive oil
1 large onion, chopped
1 cup sliced celery, with celery tops
1 clove garlic, minced
4 cups water
1 fish flavor bouillon cube
1 tablespoon salt-free Italian herb seasoning
¼ pound cod or other boneless mild-flavored fish fillets
¼ pound small shrimp, peeled and deveined
¼ pound bay scallops
1 large tomato, chopped
¼ cup flaked crabmeat or crabmeat blend
1 can (10 ounces) baby clams, rinsed and drained (optional)
2 tablespoons fresh lemon juice

1. Heat olive oil in large saucepan over medium heat until hot. Add onion, celery and garlic. Cook and stir 5 minutes or until onion is soft. Add water, bouillon cube and Italian seasoning. Cover and bring to a boil over high heat.

2. Cut cod fillets into ½-inch pieces. Add cod, shrimp, scallops and tomato to saucepan. Reduce heat and simmer 10 to 15 minutes or until seafood is opaque. Add crabmeat, clams, if desired, and lemon juice. Heat through. Garnish with lemon wedges, if desired.

makes 4 servings

prep and cook time: 30 minutes

Cioppino

Italian Sausage and Vegetable Stew

1 pound hot or mild Italian sausage links, cut into 1-inch pieces
1 package (16 ounces) frozen mixed vegetables, such as onions and green, red
    and yellow bell peppers
2 medium zucchini, sliced
1 can (14½ ounces) diced Italian-style tomatoes, undrained
1 jar (4½ ounces) sliced mushrooms, drained
4 cloves garlic, minced

1. Cook sausage in large saucepan, covered, over medium to medium-high heat 5 minutes or until browned; pour off drippings.

2. Add frozen vegetables, zucchini, tomatoes with juice, mushrooms and garlic; bring to a boil. Reduce heat and simmer, covered, 10 minutes. Cook uncovered 5 to 10 minutes or until juices have thickened slightly.

makes 6 (1-cup) servings

prep and cook time: 30 minutes

Italian Cupboard Soup

2 boneless top loin pork chops, cubed
2 (14½-ounce) cans chicken broth
1 (15-ounce) can chopped tomatoes, undrained
1 (15-ounce) can cannellini or great Northern beans, drained
2 tablespoons dried minced onion
8 ounces fresh spinach leaves, torn

In deep saucepan, brown pork in small amount of oil; add chicken broth, tomatoes, beans and onion; bring to a boil, lower heat and simmer for 15 minutes; stir in spinach and cook 2 minutes.

Top servings with grated Parmesan or Romano cheese.

makes 4 servings

Favorite recipe from **National Pork Producers Council**

Italian Sausage and Vegetable Stew

Hearty Pasta and Chick-Pea Chowder

6 ounces uncooked rotini pasta
2 tablespoons olive oil
¾ cup chopped onion
½ cup thinly sliced carrot
½ cup chopped celery
2 cloves garlic, minced
¼ cup all-purpose flour
1½ teaspoons dried Italian seasoning
⅛ teaspoon crushed red pepper
⅛ teaspoon black pepper
2 cans (13¾ ounces each) chicken broth
1 can (19 ounces) chick-peas, rinsed and drained
1 can (14½ ounces) Italian-style stewed tomatoes, undrained
6 slices bacon, cooked and crumbled

1. Cook rotini according to package directions. Rinse, drain and set aside.

2. Meanwhile, heat oil in 4-quart Dutch oven over medium-high heat until hot. Add onion, carrot, celery and garlic. Cook and stir over medium heat 5 to 6 minutes or until vegetables are crisp-tender.

3. Remove from heat. Stir in flour, Italian seasoning, red pepper and black pepper until well blended. Gradually stir in broth. Bring to a boil, stirring frequently. Boil, stirring constantly, 1 minute. Reduce heat to medium. Stir in cooked pasta, chick-peas and tomatoes. Cook 5 minutes or until heated through.

4. Sprinkle each serving with bacon. *makes 6 servings (about 7 cups)*

serving suggestion: Top with grated Parmesan cheese and serve with crusty bread, salad greens tossed with Italian dressing, and fruit cobbler.

prep and cook time: 30 minutes

Hearty Pasta and Chick-Pea Chowder

Meatball Soup

¾ pound ground turkey
1 egg white
¼ cup Italian-seasoned dry bread crumbs
3 cloves garlic, minced and divided
3 teaspoons dried Italian seasoning, divided
¾ teaspoon fennel seeds, crushed
½ teaspoon salt
⅛ teaspoon black pepper
   Olive oil-flavored nonstick cooking spray
¾ cup chopped onion
8 ounces hubbard or other winter yellow squash, peeled, seeded and cut into
   ¾-inch pieces
3 cans (14½ ounces each) fat-free reduced-sodium chicken broth
1 can (15½ ounces) Great Northern beans, rinsed and drained
2 cups chopped tomatoes
1 cup frozen peas
4 ounces uncooked ditalini pasta
   Salt and black pepper
   Minced fresh parsley

1. Preheat oven to 375°F.

2. Combine turkey, egg white, bread crumbs, 1 clove garlic, 1 teaspoon Italian seasoning, fennel seeds, ½ teaspoon salt and ⅛ teaspoon pepper in medium bowl. Shape turkey mixture into 18 meatballs.

3. Place meatballs in lightly greased baking pan and bake 15 to 20 minutes or until browned and no longer pink in center. Drain on paper towels.

4. Spray large saucepan with cooking spray; heat over medium heat until hot. Cook and stir onion, squash and remaining 2 cloves garlic about 5 minutes or until onion is tender. Add remaining 2 teaspoons Italian seasoning and cook 1 minute.

5. Add chicken broth, beans, tomatoes and peas; bring to a boil. Reduce heat and simmer, covered, 5 minutes. Add pasta and simmer, uncovered, about 10 minutes or until pasta is tender. Add meatballs during last 5 minutes of cooking time. Season to taste with salt and pepper. Ladle soup into bowls; sprinkle with parsley.   *makes 6 (2-cup) servings*

Piedmont Pork Stew

1 pound boneless pork loin, cut into 1-inch cubes
1 teaspoon vegetable oil
1 medium onion, coarsely chopped
2 carrots, sliced
8 ounces mushrooms, chopped
1 can (8 ounces) tomato sauce
1 cup dry red wine
½ cup raisins
1 teaspoon dried thyme leaves
1 teaspoon dried oregano leaves
¼ teaspoon ground cinnamon
¼ teaspoon salt
Hot cooked rice or orzo (optional)

Brown pork in oil in large pot over medium-high heat until browned, about 3 minutes. Add remaining ingredients and bring to a boil; reduce heat to a simmer, cover and cook gently 15 to 20 minutes. Serve over rice, if desired. *makes 6 servings*

preparation time: 30 minutes

Favorite recipe from **National Pork Producers Council**

Tuscan Chicken with White Beans

1 large fresh fennel bulb (about ¾ pound)
1 teaspoon olive oil
8 ounces skinless boneless chicken thighs, cut into ¾-inch pieces
1 teaspoon dried rosemary, crushed
½ teaspoon black pepper
1 can (14½ ounces) no-salt-added stewed tomatoes, undrained
1 can (about 14 ounces) reduced-sodium chicken broth
1 can (16 or 19 ounces) cannellini beans, rinsed and drained
Hot pepper sauce (optional)

1. Cut off and reserve ¼ cup chopped feathery fennel tops. Chop bulb into ½-inch pieces. Heat oil in large saucepan over medium heat. Add chopped fennel bulb; cook 5 minutes, stirring occasionally.

2. Sprinkle chicken with rosemary and pepper. Add to saucepan; cook and stir 2 minutes. Add tomatoes and chicken broth; bring to a boil. Cover and simmer 10 minutes. Stir in beans; simmer, uncovered, 15 minutes or until chicken is cooked through and sauce thickens. Season to taste with hot sauce, if desired. Ladle into shallow bowls; top with reserved fennel tops.

makes 4 servings

prep time: 15 minutes
cook time: 35 minutes

Tuscan Chicken with White Beans

Minestrone Soup

¾ cup small shell pasta
2 cans (about 14 ounces each) vegetable broth
1 can (28 ounces) crushed tomatoes in tomato purée
1 can (15 ounces) white beans, drained and rinsed
1 package (16 ounces) frozen vegetable medley, such as broccoli, green beans, carrots and red peppers
4 to 6 teaspoons prepared pesto

1. Bring 4 cups water to a boil in large saucepan over high heat. Stir in pasta; cook 8 to 10 minutes or until tender. Drain.

2. While pasta is cooking, combine broth, tomatoes and beans in Dutch oven. Cover and bring to a boil over high heat. Reduce heat to low; simmer 3 to 5 minutes.

3. Add vegetables to broth mixture and return to a boil over high heat. Stir in pasta. Simmer until vegetables and pasta are hot. Ladle soup into bowls; spoon about 1 teaspoon pesto in center of each serving.   *makes 4 to 6 servings*

prep and cook time: 20 minutes

Italian Sausage Soup

2 boxes (10 ounces each) BIRDS EYE® frozen Italian Style Vegetables & Bow-Tie Pasta
2 cans (14 ounces each) beef broth
1 pound cooked Italian sausage, cubed
1 can (8 ounces) tomato sauce

• In large saucepan, place vegetables and broth; bring to boil over high heat. Reduce heat to medium; cover and simmer 7 to 10 minutes or until vegetables are crisp-tender.

• Stir in cooked sausage and tomato sauce; cook until heated through.   *makes 4 servings*

prep time: 2 minutes
cook time: 10 to 12 minutes

Minestrone Soup

Bean and Rice Soup

3 ounces thinly sliced pancetta, chopped (about ½ cup)
1 cup chopped onion
2 quarts (four 10½-ounce cans) beef broth
2 cans (14.5 ounces each) CONTADINA® Recipe Ready Diced Tomatoes with
   Roasted Garlic, undrained
1 tablespoon chopped fresh rosemary or 1 teaspoon dried rosemary leaves,
   crushed
1 cup arborio or long-grain white rice, uncooked
¼ teaspoon salt
¼ teaspoon ground black pepper
1 can (15½ ounces) Great Northern white beans, drained
2 tablespoons chopped fresh Italian parsley

1. Sauté pancetta for 1 minute in large saucepan.

2. Add onion; sauté for 2 to 3 minutes or just until pancetta is crisp. Add broth, tomatoes with juice and rosemary. Bring to a boil.

3. Reduce heat to low; simmer, uncovered, for 10 minutes. Add rice, salt and pepper; simmer, covered, for 20 to 25 minutes or until rice is tender.

4. Add beans; simmer for 5 minutes. Sprinkle with parsley just before serving.

makes 10 cups

note: Substitute 3 bacon slices for 3 ounces pancetta.

Pesto & Tortellini Soup

1 package (9 ounces) fresh cheese tortellini
3 cans (about 14 ounces each) chicken broth
1 jar (7 ounces) roasted red peppers, drained and slivered
¾ cup frozen green peas
3 to 4 cups fresh spinach, washed and stems removed
1 to 2 tablespoons pesto

continued on page 67

Pesto & Tortellini Soup, continued

1. Cook tortellini according to package directions; drain.

2. While pasta is cooking, bring broth to a boil over high heat in covered Dutch oven. Add cooked tortellini, peppers and peas; return broth to a boil. Reduce heat to medium and simmer 1 minute.

3. Remove soup from heat; stir in spinach and pesto.   *makes 6 servings*

tip: To remove stems from spinach leaves, fold each leaf in half, then pull stem toward top of leaf. Discard stems.

prep and cook time: 14 minutes

Cioppino in a Dash

        1 tablespoon olive oil
     ½ cup green bell pepper, cut into ½-inch squares
        2 cans (14½ ounces each) no-salt-added diced tomatoes in juice, undrained
        1 can (8 ounces) no-salt-added tomato sauce
   1½ teaspoons MRS. DASH® Classic Italiano Seasoning Blend
        1 pound skinless boneless medium- or firm-flesh fish fillets (such as red snapper, cod, halibut or haddock), cut into ½-inch pieces
        8 ounces peeled, deveined shrimp
     ½ cup dry white wine

Heat oil in 3-quart saucepan over medium-high heat until hot. Cook bell pepper, stirring until tender, about 5 minutes. Add diced tomatoes, tomato sauce and seasoning. Heat to a boil; reduce heat and simmer 20 minutes. Add fish and shrimp; return to a boil. Reduce heat; cover and simmer 7 minutes or until fish and shrimp are opaque. Stir in wine during last 1 minute of cooking. Serve immediately.   *makes 6 servings*

prep time: 10 minutes
cook time: 32 minutes

Chickpea and Shrimp Soup

1 tablespoon olive or vegetable oil
1 cup diced onion
2 cloves garlic, minced
4 cans (10½ ounces each) beef broth
1 can (14½ ounces) CONTADINA® Recipe Ready Diced Tomatoes with Roasted
   Garlic, undrained
1 can (15 ounces) chickpeas or garbanzo beans, drained
1 can (6 ounces) CONTADINA® Italian Paste with Pesto
8 ounces small cooked shrimp
2 tablespoons chopped fresh Italian parsley *or* 2 teaspoons dried parsley flakes,
   crushed
½ teaspoon salt
¼ teaspoon ground black pepper

1. Heat oil over medium-high heat in large saucepan. Add onion and garlic; sauté for
1 minute.

2. Stir in broth, undrained tomatoes, chickpeas and tomato paste. Bring to boil.

3. Reduce heat to low; simmer, uncovered, 10 minutes. Add shrimp, parsley, salt and pepper;
simmer 3 minutes or until heated through. Stir before serving.   *makes 8 to 10 servings*

Chickpea and Shrimp Soup

Tuscan Vegetable Stew

        2 tablespoons olive oil
        2 teaspoons bottled minced garlic
        2 packages (4 ounces each) sliced mixed exotic mushrooms *or* 1 package
            (8 ounces) sliced button mushrooms
    ¼ cup sliced shallots or chopped sweet onion
        1 jar (7 ounces) roasted red peppers
        1 can (14½ ounces) Italian-style stewed tomatoes, undrained
        1 can (19 ounces) cannellini beans, rinsed and drained
        1 bunch fresh basil leaves*
        1 tablespoon balsamic vinegar
            Salt
            Black pepper
            Grated Romano, Parmesan or Asiago cheese

*If fresh basil is not available, add 2 teaspoons dried basil leaves to stew with tomatoes.

1. Heat oil and garlic in large deep skillet over medium heat. Add mushrooms and shallots; cook 5 minutes, stirring occasionally.

2. While mushroom mixture is cooking, drain and rinse peppers; cut into 1-inch pieces. Snip tomatoes in can into small pieces with scissors.

3. Add tomatoes, peppers and beans to skillet; bring to a boil. Reduce heat to medium-low. Cover and simmer 10 minutes, stirring once.

4. While stew is simmering, cut basil leaves into thin strips to measure ¼ cup packed. Stir basil and vinegar into stew; add salt and pepper to taste. Sprinkle each serving with cheese.

makes 4 servings

prep and cook time: 18 minutes

Tuscan Vegetable Stew

Primavera Tortellini en Brodo

    2 cans (about 14 ounces each) reduced-sodium chicken broth
    1 package (9 ounces) refrigerated fresh tortellini (cheese, chicken or sausage)
    2 cups frozen mixed vegetables, such as broccoli, green beans, onions and red
        bell peppers
    1 teaspoon dried basil leaves
      Dash hot pepper sauce or to taste
    2 teaspoons cornstarch
    1 tablespoon water
    ¼ cup grated Romano or Parmesan cheese

1. Pour broth into large deep skillet. Cover and bring to a boil over high heat. Add tortellini; reduce heat to medium-high. Cook, uncovered, until pasta is tender, stirring occasionally. (Check package directions for approximate timing.)

2. Transfer tortellini to medium bowl with slotted spoon; keep warm.

3. Add vegetables, basil and hot pepper sauce to broth; bring to a boil. Reduce heat to medium; simmer about 3 minutes or until vegetables are crisp-tender.

4. Blend cornstarch and water in small cup until smooth. Stir into broth mixture. Cook about 2 minutes or until liquid thickens slightly, stirring frequently. Return tortellini to skillet; heat through. Ladle into shallow soup bowls; sprinkle with cheese.   *makes 2 servings*

serving suggestion: Serve with salad and crusty Italian bread.

prep and cook time: 20 minutes

Primavera Tortellini en Brodo

Basil-Vegetable Soup

    1 package (9 ounces) frozen cut green beans
    1 can (15 ounces) cannellini or Great Northern beans, undrained
    3 medium carrots, thinly sliced
    3 medium zucchini or yellow squash, cut into thin slices
    2 quarts beef broth
    2 cloves garlic, minced
        Salt and pepper to taste
    2 to 3 ounces uncooked vermicelli or spaghetti
    ½ cup tightly packed fresh basil leaves, finely chopped
        Grated Romano cheese

Combine beans, carrots, zucchini, broth and garlic in Dutch oven. Bring to a boil over high heat. Reduce heat to low. Cover; simmer until carrots are tender. Season with salt and pepper. Add vermicelli; bring to a boil over high heat. Reduce heat to low. Simmer until pasta is tender, yet firm. (Pasta may be cooked separately; add to soup just before serving.) Add basil; simmer until basil is tender. Serve with cheese.   *makes 10 to 12 servings*

Tuscany Chicken Soup

    4½ cups water
     1 package LIPTON® Noodles & Sauce—Chicken Flavor
     1 package (8 ounces) frozen Italian vegetables, partially thawed
     1 can (14½ ounces) whole peeled tomatoes, undrained and chopped
    1½ teaspoons garlic powder
     1 teaspoon oregano leaves
     2 cups cut-up cooked chicken
    ¼ cup grated Parmesan cheese
        Salt and ground black pepper to taste

In 3-quart saucepan, bring water to a boil. Stir in noodles & sauce—chicken flavor, vegetables, tomatoes, garlic powder and oregano. Cover and return to a boil. Uncover and continue boiling over medium heat, stirring occasionally, 8 minutes or until noodles and vegetables are tender. Stir in remaining ingredients and heat through.

makes about 4 (2-cup) servings

Hearty Minestrone Gratiné

1 cup diced celery
1 cup diced zucchini
1 can (28 ounces) tomatoes with liquid, chopped
2 cups water
2 teaspoons sugar
1 teaspoon dried Italian herb seasoning
1 can (15 ounces) garbanzo beans, drained
4 (½-inch) slices French bread, toasted
1 cup (4 ounces) SARGENTO® Light Mozzarella Shredded Cheese
2 tablespoons SARGENTO® Fancy Parmesan Shredded Cheese
Freshly chopped parsley

Spray a large saucepan or Dutch oven with nonstick cooking spray. Over medium heat, sauté celery and zucchini until tender. Add tomatoes, water, sugar and herb seasoning. Simmer, uncovered, 15 to 20 minutes. Add garbanzo beans and heat an additional 10 minutes. Meanwhile, heat broiler. Place toasted French bread on broiler pan. Top with Mozzarella cheese. Broil until cheese melts. Ladle soup into bowls and top with French bread. Sprinkle Parmesan cheese over each bowl and garnish with parsley. Serve immediately.

makes 4 servings

Shellfish Cioppino

    12 cherrystone clams
       Salt
     4 tablespoons olive oil
     2 cups chopped onions
     2 red bell peppers, seeded and chopped
     1 green bell pepper, seeded and chopped
     8 cloves garlic, minced
     2 cups fish stock or bottled clam juice
     2 cups vermouth or white wine
     2 cans (16 ounces each) tomatoes, drained and coarsely chopped
     1 tablespoon dried basil leaves
     1 teaspoon dried thyme leaves
     1 bay leaf
    ¼ teaspoon red pepper flakes
    ¾ pound raw large shrimp, peeled and deveined
    ½ pound sea scallops
     8 crab claws or claw-shaped surimi

1. To prepare clams,* discard any clams that remain open when tapped with fingers. To clean clams, scrub with stiff brush under cold running water. Soak clams in mixture of ⅓ cup salt to 1 gallon water 20 minutes. Drain water; repeat 2 more times.

2. To steam clams, place 1 cup water in large stockpot. Bring to a boil over high heat. Add clams. Cover stockpot; reduce heat to medium. Steam 5 to 7 minutes or until clams open. Remove from stockpot with tongs; set aside. Discard any clams that remain unopened.

3. Heat oil in stockpot over medium-high heat. Add onions, bell peppers and garlic. Cover; reduce heat to low. Cook 20 to 25 minutes or until tender, stirring occasionally.

4. Add fish stock, vermouth, tomatoes, basil, thyme, bay leaf and red pepper. Partly cover; simmer 30 minutes.

5. Add clams, shrimp, scallops and crab claws. Cover; remove from heat. Let stand until shrimp and scallops turn opaque. Remove bay leaf; discard. Ladle into large bowls.

makes 4 generous servings

*Substitute ½ pint shucked clams for clams in shells. Steam in steamer until firm. Omit steps 1 and 2.

Shellfish Cioppino

HEARTY PASTA DISHES

Chicken and Linguine in Creamy Tomato Sauce

1 tablespoon olive or vegetable oil
1 pound boneless, skinless chicken breasts, cut into ½-inch strips
1 jar (26 to 28 ounces) RAGÚ® Old World Style® Pasta Sauce
2 cups water
8 ounces linguine or spaghetti
½ cup whipping or heavy cream
1 tablespoon fresh basil leaves, chopped *or* ½ teaspoon dried basil leaves, crushed

1. In 12-inch skillet, heat oil over medium heat and brown chicken. Remove chicken and set aside.

2. In same skillet, stir in Ragú Pasta Sauce and water. Bring to a boil over high heat. Stir in uncooked linguine and return to a boil. Reduce heat to low and simmer covered, stirring occasionally, 15 minutes or until linguine is tender.

3. Stir in cream and basil. Return chicken to skillet and cook 5 minutes or until chicken is no longer pink.

makes 4 servings

prep time: 10 minutes
cook time: 30 minutes

Chicken and Linguine in Creamy
Tomato Sauce

Mafalda and Meatballs

    1 teaspoon olive oil
    2 cloves garlic, minced, divided
    2 cans (14½ ounces each) no-salt-added stewed tomatoes, undrained
    ½ teaspoon dried basil leaves
    8 ounces lean ground beef
    8 ounces lean ground turkey
    ⅓ cup dry French bread crumbs
    3 tablespoons fat-free reduced-sodium chicken broth
    3 tablespoons cholesterol-free egg substitute
    1 teaspoon fennel seeds
    ¼ teaspoon salt
    ⅛ teaspoon black pepper
    8 ounces uncooked mafalda or spaghetti noodles

1. Heat oil in large nonstick saucepan over medium-high heat. Add half of garlic; cook 1 minute. Add tomatoes with juice and basil; bring to a boil. Reduce heat. Simmer, uncovered, 20 to 25 minutes or until sauce thickens, stirring occasionally.

2. Meanwhile, combine beef, turkey, bread crumbs, chicken broth, egg substitute, fennel seeds, remaining half of garlic, salt and pepper in large bowl; mix well. With wet hands, shape meat mixture into 12 (1-inch) balls.

3. Preheat broiler. Spray broiler pan with nonstick cooking spray. Arrange meatballs on broiler pan. Broil, 4 inches from heat, 10 minutes or until no longer pink in center. Remove and add to tomato mixture. Cover; cook 5 to 10 minutes or until heated through.

4. Cook noodles according to package directions. Drain. Arrange noodles on serving platter. Pour meatballs and sauce over pasta. Serve with shredded Parmesan cheese, if desired.

makes 4 servings

Mafalda and Meatballs

Italian Sausage with Pesto & Pasta

½ cup packed basil leaves
¼ cup plus 2 tablespoons walnut pieces, toasted and divided
2 cloves garlic, peeled
¼ cup grated Parmesan cheese
5 tablespoons olive oil
1 package (12 ounces) uncooked linguine
1 pound cooked Italian sausage links, sliced
2 cups broccoli florets

Combine basil, ¼ cup walnuts and garlic in food processor or blender container; process until smooth. Add cheese. With machine running, pour oil through feed tube and process until ingredients are well blended; set aside.

Prepare pasta according to package directions. During last 2 minutes of cooking, add sausage and broccoli to pasta; drain. Combine pasta mixture with pesto. Season to taste with salt and pepper. Garnish with remaining 2 tablespoons walnuts. .   *makes 6 servings*

Spinach Tortellini with Bel Paese®

2 tablespoons butter
4 ounces BEL PAESE® Cheese,* cut into small chunks
¾ cup half-and-half
3 ounces chopped GALBANI® Prosciutto di Parma
   Pepper
8 ounces spinach tortellini

Remove wax coating and moist, white crust from cheese.

In small saucepan, melt butter over low heat. Add Bel Paese® Cheese and half-and-half; cook until smooth, stirring constantly. Stir in Galbani® Prosciutto di Parma; sprinkle with pepper to taste. Remove from heat; set aside.

In large saucepan of boiling water, cook tortellini until al dente (tender but still firm); drain. Place in serving bowl. Pour sauce over pasta; toss to coat. Serve immediately.

makes 2 servings

Italian Sausage with Pesto & Pasta

Ravioli with Creamy Spinach Sauce

1 package (24 ounces) frozen beef ravioli
1 box (10 ounces) BIRDS EYE® frozen Chopped Spinach
1 jar (14½ ounces) alfredo pasta sauce*
¼ teaspoon ground nutmeg
1 cup chopped tomato or roasted red pepper

*Or, substitute 1 packet (1.6 ounces) alfredo pasta sauce mix prepared according to package directions.

• In large saucepan, cook ravioli according to package directions; drain and set aside.

• Cook spinach according to package directions; place in strainer. Press excess water from spinach with back of spoon.

• In same saucepan, place spinach, alfredo sauce and nutmeg; cook over medium heat until heated through.

• Add ravioli and tomato; toss together.   *makes 4 servings*

serving suggestion: Serve with a marinated tomato salad.

prep time: 5 minutes
cook time: 20 minutes

Ravioli with Creamy Spinach Sauce

Lasagna Supreme

8 ounces lasagna noodles
½ pound ground beef
½ pound mild Italian sausage, casings removed
1 medium onion, chopped
2 cloves garlic, minced
1 can (14½ ounces) whole tomatoes, undrained and chopped
1 can (6 ounces) tomato paste
2 teaspoons dried basil leaves
1 teaspoon dried marjoram leaves
1 can (4 ounces) sliced mushrooms, drained
2 eggs
1 pound cream-style cottage cheese
¾ cup grated Parmesan cheese, divided
2 tablespoons dried parsley flakes
½ teaspoon salt
½ teaspoon black pepper
2 cups (8 ounces) shredded Cheddar cheese
3 cups (12 ounces) shredded mozzarella cheese

1. Cook lasagna noodles according to package directions; drain.

2. Cook meats, onion and garlic in large skillet over medium-high heat until meat is brown, stirring to separate meat. Drain.

3. Add tomatoes with juice, tomato paste, basil and marjoram. Reduce heat to low. Cover; simmer 15 minutes, stirring often. Stir in mushrooms; set aside.

4. Preheat oven to 375°F. Beat eggs in large bowl; add cottage cheese, ½ cup Parmesan cheese, parsley, salt and pepper. Mix well.

5. Place half the noodles in bottom of 13×9-inch baking pan. Spread half the cottage cheese mixture over noodles, then half the meat mixture and half the Cheddar cheese and mozzarella cheese. Repeat layers. Sprinkle with remaining ¼ cup Parmesan cheese.

6. Bake lasagna 40 to 45 minutes or until bubbly. Let stand 10 minutes before cutting.

makes 8 to 10 servings

note: Lasagna may be assembled, covered and refrigerated up to 2 days in advance. Bake, uncovered, in preheated 375°F oven 60 minutes or until bubbly.

Turkey Stuffed Pasta Italiano

1 pound ground California turkey
1 cup minced onion
1 cup grated peeled eggplant
2 cloves garlic, minced
   Salt and pepper
1 can (28 ounces) tomatoes, undrained
1 can (8 ounces) tomato sauce
1 cup red wine or water
1 teaspoon garlic salt
1 teaspoon dried oregano leaves
1 teaspoon dried basil leaves
½ teaspoon dried tarragon leaves
½ teaspoon crushed red pepper
1 package (12 ounces) uncooked jumbo pasta shells
½ cup grated Parmesan cheese
¾ cup (3 ounces) shredded mozzarella cheese

In large nonstick skillet, brown turkey, onion, eggplant and garlic until turkey is no longer pink; drain. Season with salt and pepper; reserve. In small saucepan, simmer tomatoes with juice, tomato sauce, wine and seasonings for 15 minutes. Cook pasta shells until done, but still firm; drain. In large bowl, combine turkey mixture and Parmesan cheese with half the tomato sauce mixture. Stuff shells; place in 13×9-inch pan. Spoon remaining sauce mixture over shells; top with mozzarella cheese. Bake at 350°F for 30 minutes.

makes 8 to 10 servings

Favorite recipe from **California Poultry Federation**

Tip

Shells can be stuffed ahead of time and refrigerated. Add sauce and mozzarella cheese just before baking. Increase cooking time by 8 to 10 minutes.

Spaghetti alla Bolognese

        2 tablespoons olive oil
        1 medium onion, chopped
        1 pound ground beef
        ½ small carrot, finely chopped
        ½ rib celery, finely chopped
        1 cup dry white wine
        ½ cup milk
        ⅛ teaspoon ground nutmeg
        1 can (14½ ounces) whole peeled tomatoes, undrained and coarsely chopped
        1 cup beef broth
        3 tablespoons tomato paste
        1 teaspoon salt
        1 teaspoon dried basil leaves
        ½ teaspoon dried thyme leaves
        ⅛ teaspoon black pepper
        1 bay leaf
        1 pound uncooked spaghetti
        1 cup freshly grated Parmesan cheese (about 3 ounces)

1. Heat oil in large skillet over medium heat. Cook and stir onion until soft. Crumble beef into onion mixture. Brown 6 minutes, stirring to separate meat, or until meat just loses its pink color. Spoon off and discard fat.

2. Stir carrot and celery into meat mixture; cook 2 minutes over medium-high heat. Stir in wine; cook 4 to 6 minutes until wine has evaporated. Stir in milk and nutmeg; reduce heat to medium and cook 3 to 4 minutes until milk has almost evaporated. Remove from heat.

3. Press tomatoes with juice through sieve into meat mixture; discard seeds.

4. Stir beef broth, tomato paste, salt, basil, thyme, pepper and bay leaf into meat mixture. Bring to a boil; reduce heat and simmer, uncovered, 1 to 1½ hours until most of liquid has evaporated and sauce thickens, stirring frequently. Remove and discard bay leaf.

5. Cook spaghetti in large pot of boiling salted water according to package directions just until al dente; drain well. Combine hot spaghetti and meat sauce in serving bowl; toss lightly. Sprinkle with cheese. Garnish with thyme sprig, if desired.   *makes 4 to 6 servings*

Spaghetti alla Bolognese

Chicken Tetrazzini with Roasted Red Peppers

6 ounces uncooked egg noodles
3 tablespoons butter or margarine
¼ cup all-purpose flour
1 can (14½ ounces) chicken broth
1 cup whipping cream
2 tablespoons dry sherry
2 cans (6 ounces each) sliced mushrooms, drained
1 jar (7½ ounces) roasted red peppers, drained and cut into ½-inch strips
2 cups chopped cooked chicken
1 teaspoon dried Italian seasoning
½ cup (2 ounces) grated Parmesan cheese

1. Cook egg noodles according to package directions. Drain well.

2. While noodles are cooking, melt butter in medium saucepan over medium heat. Add flour and whisk until smooth. Add chicken broth; bring to a boil over high heat. Remove from heat. Gradually add whipping cream and sherry; stir to combine.

3. Combine mushrooms, red peppers and noodles in large bowl; toss to combine. Add half the chicken broth mixture to noodle mixture. Combine remaining chicken broth mixture, chicken and Italian seasoning in large bowl.

4. Spoon noodle mixture into serving dish. Make a well in center of noodles and spoon in chicken mixture. Sprinkle cheese over top.

makes 6 servings

prep and cook time: 20 minutes

Chicken Tetrazzini with Roasted
Red Peppers

Penne with Shrimp and Vegetables

        2 tablespoons olive or vegetable oil
        2 medium zucchini, cut into 2-inch strips (about 2 cups)
        1 tablespoon minced shallots
        8 ounces medium shrimp, peeled, deveined
        1 medium yellow bell pepper, cut into 2-inch strips (about 1 cup)
        1 can (14.5-ounce can) CONTADINA® Recipe Ready Diced Tomatoes with
            Roasted Garlic, undrained
        1 cup sliced pitted ripe olives, drained
        1 tablespoon capers
        8 ounces dry penne pasta, cooked, drained, kept warm

1. Heat oil in large skillet. Add zucchini and shallots; sauté 1 to 2 minutes or until zucchini are crisp-tender.

2. Add shrimp and bell pepper; sauté 2 to 4 minutes or until shrimp turn pink.

3. Stir in undrained tomatoes, olives and capers; simmer, uncovered, 2 minutes. Serve over pasta.   *makes 6 servings*

Tagliatelle with Creamy Sauce

        7 to 8 ounces tagliatelle pasta, cooked, drained
        1 cup GALBANI® Mascarpone cheese
        1 package (10 ounces) frozen peas, cooked, drained
        2 ounces (½ cup) finely chopped GALBANI® Prosciutto di Parma
    1½ cups (6 ounces) shredded mozzarella cheese
        Butter or margarine

Layer ½ of the tagliatelle in buttered 9×9-inch baking dish. Spoon ½ of the Mascarpone onto tagliatelle. Sprinkle with ½ of the peas and ½ of the prosciutto. Top with ½ of the mozzarella. Repeat layers. Dot with butter. Bake in preheated 350°F oven 20 minutes or until heated through.   *makes 4 to 6 servings*

Penne with Shrimp and Vegetables

Fettuccine alla Carbonara

¾ pound uncooked fettuccine or spaghetti
4 ounces pancetta (Italian bacon) or lean American bacon, cut into ½-inch-wide strips
3 cloves garlic, cut into halves
¼ cup dry white wine
⅓ cup heavy or whipping cream
1 egg
1 egg yolk
⅔ cup freshly grated Parmesan cheese, divided
Generous dash white pepper
Fresh oregano leaves for garnish

1. Cook fettuccine in large pot of boiling salted water according to package directions just until al dente; remove from heat. Drain well; return to dry pot.

2. Cook and stir pancetta and garlic in large skillet over medium-low heat 4 minutes or until pancetta is light brown. Reserve 2 tablespoons drippings in skillet with pancetta. Discard garlic and remaining drippings.

3. Add wine to pancetta mixture; cook over medium heat 3 minutes or until wine is almost evaporated. Stir in cream; cook and stir 2 minutes. Remove from heat.

4. Whisk egg and egg yolk in top of double boiler. Place top of double boiler over simmering water, adjusting heat to maintain simmer. Whisk ⅓ cup cheese and pepper into egg mixture; cook and stir until sauce thickens slightly.

5. Pour pancetta mixture over fettuccine in pot; toss to coat. Heat over medium-low heat until heated through. Stir in egg mixture. Toss to coat evenly. Remove from heat. Serve with remaining ⅓ cup cheese. Garnish, if desired. *makes 4 servings*

Fettuccine alla Carbonara

Spaghetti with Seafood Marinara Sauce

    8 fresh oysters
    2 tablespoons olive oil
    ⅓ cup chopped onion
    1 clove garlic, minced
    ½ cup dry white wine
    6 flat anchovy fillets, minced
    5 large ripe fresh tomatoes, seeded and chopped
    1 tablespoon tomato paste
    ¾ teaspoon salt
    ¾ teaspoon dried basil
    ½ teaspoon dried oregano
    ⅛ teaspoon black pepper
   10 ounces uncooked spaghetti
    1 pound fresh medium shrimp, shelled and deveined
    ½ pound fresh sea scallops, cut into ¾-inch pieces
    3 tablespoons chopped fresh parsley
      Fresh basil leaves for garnish

1. Scrub oysters thoroughly with stiff brush under cold running water. Place on tray and refrigerate 1 hour to help oysters relax.

2. Shuck oysters, reserving oyster liquor. Strain oyster liquor through triple thickness of dampened cheesecloth into small bowl; reserve oyster liquor.

3. Heat oil in 3-quart saucepan over medium-high heat. Add onion; cook and stir 4 minutes or until soft. Add garlic; cook 30 seconds. Add wine; cook 4 to 5 minutes until wine has evaporated. Remove from heat; cover and set aside.

4. Stir reserved oyster liquor and anchovies into onion mixture in saucepan; add tomatoes, tomato paste, salt, basil, oregano and pepper. Mix well. Bring to a boil over high heat; reduce heat to medium. Cook, uncovered, 20 minutes or until sauce thickens, stirring occasionally.

5. Cook spaghetti according to package directions just until al dente; drain well.

continued on page 97

6. Stir shrimp, scallops and oysters into marinara sauce. Cover and cook 2 to 3 minutes until shrimp turn opaque and are cooked through, stirring occasionally. Stir in parsley.

7. Combine hot spaghetti with seafood sauce in large serving bowl; toss until well coated. Garnish, if desired. Serve immediately. *makes 4 to 5 servings*

note: Oysters should have tightly closed shells or snap tightly closed when tapped. If they do not close when tapped, they are dead and should be discarded.

Zucchini Pasta Bake

1½ cups uncooked pasta tubes
½ pound ground beef
½ cup chopped onion
1 clove garlic, minced
Salt and pepper
1 can (14½ ounces) DEL MONTE® Zucchini with Italian-Style Tomato Sauce
1 teaspoon dried basil, crushed
1 cup (4 ounces) shredded Monterey Jack cheese

1. Cook pasta according to package directions; drain.

2. Cook beef with onion and garlic in large skillet; drain. Season with salt and pepper.

3. Stir in zucchini with tomato sauce and basil. Place pasta in 8-inch square baking dish. Top with meat mixture.

4. Bake at 350°F for 15 minutes. Top with cheese. Bake 3 minutes or until cheese is melted.
makes 4 servings

prep and cook time: 33 minutes

Chicken Pesto Mozzarella

6 to 8 ounces linguine or corkscrew pasta
4 boneless, skinless chicken breasts halves
1 tablespoon olive oil
1 can (14½ ounces) DEL MONTE® Diced Tomatoes with Basil, Garlic & Oregano, undrained
½ medium onion, chopped
⅓ cup sliced ripe olives
4 teaspoons pesto sauce*
¼ cup (1 ounce) shredded mozzarella cheese

Pesto sauce is available frozen or refrigerated at the supermarket.

1. Cook pasta according to package directions; drain.

2. Meanwhile, season chicken with salt and pepper, if desired. In large skillet, brown chicken in hot oil over medium-high heat. Add tomatoes, onion and olives; bring to boil. Cover and cook 8 minutes over medium heat.

3. Remove cover; cook about 8 minutes or until chicken is no longer pink in center.

4. Spread 1 teaspoon pesto over each chicken breast; top with cheese. Cover and cook until cheese is melted. Serve over pasta. Garnish, if desired.   *makes 4 servings*

prep time: 10 minutes
cook time: 25 minutes

Chicken Pesto Mozzarella

Turkey Sausage & Pasta Toss

8 ounces uncooked penne or gemelli pasta
1 can (14½ ounces) no-salt-added stewed tomatoes, undrained
6 ounces turkey kielbasa or smoked turkey sausage
2 cups fresh asparagus pieces (1 inch) or broccoli florets
2 tablespoons prepared reduced-fat pesto sauce
2 tablespoons grated Parmesan cheese

1. Cook pasta according to package directions, omitting salt.

2. Meanwhile, heat tomatoes with juice in medium saucepan. Cut sausage crosswise into ¼-inch slices; add to tomatoes. Stir in asparagus and pesto; cover and simmer about 6 minutes or until asparagus is crisp-tender.

3. Drain pasta; toss with tomato mixture and sprinkle with cheese.   *makes 4 servings*

prep and cook time: 25 minutes

Creamy Garlic Clam Sauce with Linguine

1 jar (16 ounces) RAGÚ® Cheese Creations!® Roasted Garlic Parmesan Sauce
2 cans (6½ ounces each) chopped clams, undrained
1 tablespoon chopped fresh parsley *or* ½ teaspoon dried parsley flakes
8 ounces linguine or spaghetti, cooked and drained

1. In 3-quart saucepan, cook Ragú Cheese Creations! Sauce, clams and parsley over medium heat, stirring occasionally, 10 minutes.

2. Serve over hot linguine and garnish, if desired, with fresh lemon wedges.

makes 4 servings

prep time: 5 minutes
cook time: 15 minutes

Turkey Sausage & Pasta Toss

Lasagna

1 teaspoon olive oil
2 cloves garlic, minced
2 cans (14 ounces each) no-salt-added Italian-style tomatoes, undrained
½ teaspoon dried Italian seasoning
8 ounces lean ground beef
1 large onion, chopped
8 ounces fresh mushrooms, sliced
2 zucchini, shredded
8 ounces uncooked lasagna noodles
1 cup 1% low-fat cottage cheese
1 cup nonfat ricotta cheese
1 cup (4 ounces) shredded part-skim mozzarella cheese, divided
2 egg whites
2 tablespoons Parmesan cheese

1. Heat oil in large nonstick skillet over medium heat. Add garlic; cook 1 minute. Add tomatoes with juice and seasoning; bring to a boil. Reduce heat; simmer, uncovered, 20 to 25 minutes or until sauce thickens.

2. Heat large nonstick skillet over medium heat. Add beef and onion; cook and stir until beef is browned and onion is tender. Drain. Stir in mushrooms and zucchini; cook and stir 5 to 10 minutes or until tender.

3. Cook noodles according to package directions, omitting salt. Drain. Rinse under cold water; drain well. Combine cottage cheese, ricotta cheese, ½ cup mozzarella cheese and egg whites in medium bowl.

4. Preheat oven to 350°F. Spray 13×9-inch baking pan with nonstick cooking spray. Place layer of noodles in bottom of pan. Spread half of beef mixture over noodles. Top with half of cheese mixture and noodles. Repeat layering process, ending with noodles. Pour tomato mixture over noodles. Sprinkle with remaining ½ cup mozzarella and Parmesan cheese. Cover; bake 30 minutes. Uncover; bake 10 to 15 minutes or until heated through. Let stand 10 minutes before serving. Garnish as desired.

makes 8 servings

Lasagna

Tuscan Noodle Bake

½ pound Italian sausage, casings removed and sausage crumbled
½ pound ground turkey
1 cup chopped onion
1 teaspoon fresh minced garlic
1 (15-ounce) can HUNT'S® Tomato Sauce
1 (7½-ounce) can HUNT'S® Whole Tomatoes, undrained and crushed
1 (6-ounce) can sliced mushrooms, drained
1 (2¼-ounce) can sliced black olives, drained
¼ cup chopped fresh parsley
1 teaspoon dried basil
1 teaspoon dried oregano leaves
¼ teaspoon pepper
¼ cup grated Parmesan cheese
½ (12-ounce) package wide egg noodles, cooked and drained
1 cup shredded mozzarella cheese

In large Dutch oven, brown sausage and turkey with onion and garlic until meat is no longer pink; drain. Add remaining ingredients except Parmesan cheese, noodles and mozzarella cheese; simmer 5 minutes. Stir in Parmesan cheese and noodles; blend well. Pour noodle mixture into greased 13×9×2-inch baking dish. Bake, covered, at 350°F for 20 minutes. Sprinkle mozzarella cheese over noodle mixture and bake, uncovered, for an additional 5 to 7 minutes.

makes 6 to 8 servings

Tip

Italian sausage is traditionally seasoned with fennel seed, which gives it a distinctive flavor. Two versions, mild or sweet and hot, are available.

Porcini Mushroom Penne Pasta in Pesto Sauce

    1 (10-ounce) package PASTA LABELLA™ Porcini Mushroom Penne
    ¼ cup Pesto (recipe follows)
    ¼ cup olive oil
    ¾ pound Genoa salami, julienned
    2 cups thinly sliced assorted mushrooms (porcini, portabella or white)
    ½ cup chopped roasted red peppers
    ½ cup beef consommé or beef broth
    3 cups heavy cream
    2 ounces Chèvre cheese
    ¼ cup grated Parmesan cheese
    ¼ cup grated Romano cheese
       Salt and ground black pepper to taste
    2 tablespoons thinly sliced green onion

Prepare Pesto.

Cook pasta according to package directions. Drain and keep warm; set aside.

Heat olive oil in large skillet over high heat until hot. Add salami, mushrooms, roasted red peppers and Pesto. Cook and stir 2 minutes. Add cooked pasta; cook and stir 2 minutes. Add consommé; cook 1 minute. Add heavy cream, Chèvre, Parmesan and Romano cheeses; cook until slightly thickened. Add salt and black pepper to taste. Garnish with green onion.

makes 4 servings

Pesto

    1 cup fresh basil leaves
    1 cup fresh parsley
    ¼ cup pine nuts, toasted
    3 tablespoons chopped garlic
    ½ cup olive oil
    ¾ cup grated Parmesan cheese

Place basil, parsley, toasted pine nuts and garlic in food processor or blender. Process until mixture is finely chopped. With processor running, add olive oil in slow steady stream until evenly blended. Stir in Parmesan cheese; blend well.

Linguine with Clam Sauce

8 ounces uncooked linguine
2 tablespoons olive oil
1 cup chopped onions
1 can (14½ ounces) stewed Italian-style tomatoes, drained and chopped
2 cloves garlic, minced
2 teaspoons dried basil leaves
½ cup dry white wine or chicken broth
1 can (10 ounces) whole baby clams, drained, juice reserved
⅓ cup chopped fresh parsley
¼ teaspoon salt
¼ teaspoon black pepper

1. Cook linguine according to package directions. Rinse, drain and set aside.

2. Meanwhile, heat oil in large skillet over medium heat until hot. Add onions; cook and stir 3 minutes. Add tomatoes, garlic and basil; cook and stir 3 minutes. Stir in wine and reserved clam juice; bring to a boil and simmer, uncovered, 5 minutes.

3. Stir in clams, parsley, salt and pepper. Cook 1 to 2 minutes or until heated through. Spoon over linguine. Serve immediately. *makes 4 servings*

serving suggestion: Serve with steamed broccoli florets tossed in Italian salad dressing, sliced crusty bread and spumone.

prep and cook time: 20 minutes

Tip

The easiest way to peel garlic cloves is to trim off the ends and lightly crush the cloves with the flat side of a chef's knife. The peels can then be easily removed.

Linguine with Clam Sauce

Creamy Chicken Primavera

1 teaspoon olive or vegetable oil
2 medium red, yellow or green bell peppers, coarsely chopped
1 medium onion, chopped
1 pound boneless, skinless chicken breasts, cut into 1-inch pieces
½ cup frozen green peas, thawed
1 jar (16 ounces) RAGÚ® Cheese Creations!® Light Parmesan Alfredo Sauce
⅛ teaspoon ground black pepper
8 ounces linguine or spaghetti, cooked and drained

1. In 12-inch nonstick skillet, heat oil over medium-high heat and cook red bell peppers and onion, stirring occasionally, 10 minutes or until golden.

2. Stir in chicken and peas and continue cooking, stirring occasionally, 5 minutes. Stir in Ragú Cheese Creations! Sauce and black pepper.

3. Reduce heat to medium and simmer, stirring occasionally, 10 minutes or until chicken is no longer pink. Serve over hot linguine. *makes 4 servings*

prep time: 15 minutes
cook time: 30 minutes

Creamy Chicken Primavera

Prego® Quick Skillet Ziti

1 pound ground beef
1 jar (28 ounces) PREGO® Traditional Pasta Sauce
5 cups cooked medium tube-shaped macaroni (about 3 cups uncooked)
  Grated Parmesan cheese

1. In medium skillet over medium-high heat, cook beef until browned, stirring to separate meat. Pour off fat.

2. Add pasta sauce and macaroni. Reduce heat to low and heat through. Serve with cheese.

makes 5 servings

note: For a shortcut supper on a busy day, try PREGO® Spaghetti & Meatballs. In a large saucepan mix 1 jar (28 ounces) PREGO® Traditional Pasta Sauce with 12 frozen *or* refrigerated fully cooked meatballs (about 12 ounces). Over medium heat, heat to a boil. Reduce heat to low. Cover and cook about 15 minutes or until meatballs are heated through, stirring occasionally. Serve over 4 cups hot cooked spaghetti (about 8 ounces uncooked). Makes 4 servings

prep time: 10 minutes
cook time: 15 minutes

Tip

Ziti, penne, mostaccioli and rigatoni are examples of tube-shaped pasta. Elbow macaroni can be substituted in this recipe.

Prego® Quick Skillet Ziti

Linguine with Tuna Antipasto

1 package (9 ounces) uncooked refrigerated flavored linguine, such as tomato and herb
1 can (6 ounces) tuna in water, drained and broken into pieces
1 jar (6½ ounces) marinated artichoke hearts, coarsely chopped and liquid reserved
½ cup roasted red peppers, drained and coarsely chopped
⅓ cup olive oil
¼ cup coarsely chopped black olives
½ teaspoon minced garlic
¼ teaspoon salt
¼ teaspoon red pepper flakes
⅛ teaspoon black pepper
½ cup grated Parmesan cheese

1. Cook linguine according to package directions.

2. While linguine is cooking, combine remaining ingredients except cheese in large microwavable bowl. Mix well; cover with vented plastic wrap. Microwave at HIGH 2 to 3 minutes or until heated through.

3. Drain linguine; add to bowl. Toss well; arrange on 4 plates. Sprinkle with cheese; garnish as desired.   *makes 4 servings*

prep and cook time: 18 minutes

Tip

Parmesan cheese is a hard Italian cheese that has been aged. It is available pregrated and in blocks for grating just before use. Freshly grated Parmesan cheese has more flavor.

Linguini with Tuna Antipasto

Chicken Tortellini with Mushroom-Cream Sauce

2 cups plus 1 tablespoon all-purpose flour
½ teaspoon salt, divided
4 eggs
1 tablespoon milk
1 teaspoon olive oil
2 small boneless skinless chicken breast halves, cooked and minced
2 ounces fresh spinach, cooked, squeezed dry and minced
2 ounces prosciutto or cooked ham, minced
⅓ cup plus 2 tablespoons grated Parmesan cheese, divided
2 cups heavy or whipping cream (1 pint), divided
  Dash pepper
3 tablespoons butter or margarine
½ pound fresh mushrooms, thinly sliced
3 tablespoons chopped fresh parsley

1. Combine flour and ¼ teaspoon salt on pastry board, cutting board or countertop; make well in center. Whisk 3 eggs, milk and oil in small bowl until well blended; gradually pour into well in flour mixture while mixing with fingertips or fork to form ball of dough.

2. Place dough on lightly floured surface; flatten slightly. To knead dough, fold dough in half toward you and press dough away from you with heels of hands. Give dough a quarter turn and continue folding, pushing and turning. Continue kneading 5 minutes or until smooth and elastic, adding more flour to prevent sticking if necessary. Wrap dough in plastic wrap; set aside. Allow dough to stand at least 15 minutes.

3. Combine chicken, spinach, prosciutto and remaining egg in medium bowl; mix well. Add 2 tablespoons cheese, 1 tablespoon cream, remaining ¼ teaspoon salt and pepper to spinach mixture; mix well.

4. Unwrap dough and knead briefly (as described in step 2) on lightly floured surface; divide into 3 pieces. Using lightly floured rolling pin, roll out 1 dough piece to 1/16-inch thickness on lightly floured surface. (Keep remaining dough pieces wrapped in plastic wrap to prevent drying.) Cut out dough circles with 2-inch round cutter. Cover rolled dough with clean kitchen towel to prevent drying while working.

continued on page 115

114

5. Place ½ teaspoon chicken filling in center of 1 dough circle; brush edge of circle lightly with water. Fold circle in half to enclose filling, making sure all air has been pushed out. Pinch outside edges together firmly to seal.

6. Brush end of half circle with water; wrap around finger overlapping ends. Pinch to seal. Place tortellini on clean kitchen towel. Repeat with remaining dough circles, rerolling dough scraps as needed. Repeat with remaining 2 dough pieces and chicken filling. Let tortellini dry on towel for 30 minutes before cooking.

7. Heat butter in 3-quart saucepan over medium heat until melted and bubbly; cook and stir mushrooms in hot butter 3 minutes. Stir in remaining cream. Bring to a boil over medium heat; immediately reduce heat to low. Simmer, uncovered, 3 minutes. Stir in remaining ⅓ cup cheese; cook and stir 1 minute. Remove from heat.

8. Cook tortellini, ⅓ at a time, in large pot of boiling salted water 2 to 3 minutes just until al dente. Drain well; add to mushroom-cream sauce. Bring mushroom-cream sauce and tortellini just to a boil over medium heat; reduce heat to low. Simmer 2 minutes. Sprinkle with parsley. Serve immediately. *makes 6 to 8 servings*

Manicotti alla Perdue

2 cups finely chopped cooked PERDUE® Chicken or Turkey
1 container (15 ounces) ricotta cheese
1 egg, slightly beaten
1 package (10 ounces) frozen chopped spinach, thawed and well drained
¼ cup grated Parmesan cheese
½ teaspoon ground nutmeg
3 cups marinara or spaghetti sauce, divided
1 package (8 ounces) manicotti shells, cooked
½ to ¾ cup shredded mozzarella cheese

Preheat oven to 350°F. In medium bowl, combine first 6 ingredients. Into 12×9-inch baking pan, spoon a thin layer of marinara sauce. Fill manicotti shells with chicken or turkey mixture and arrange over sauce. Pour remaining sauce on top; sprinkle with mozzarella. Bake 25 to 30 minutes until hot and bubbly. *makes 4 to 6 servings*

Crispy Italian Herb Chicken with Tri-Color Rotini Pasta

2 BUTTERBALL® Chicken Requests™ Italian Style Herb Crispy Baked Breasts
1 cup uncooked tri-color rotini pasta
3 tablespoons water
1 tablespoon olive oil
2 cups broccoli florets
3 plum tomatoes, quartered
1 clove garlic, minced
   Grated Parmesan cheese

Prepare chicken according to package directions. Cook and drain pasta. Add water, oil and broccoli to skillet; cover. Cook 2 to 4 minutes. Stir in pasta, tomatoes and garlic; continue cooking 2 minutes longer. Serve chicken breasts with pasta. Sprinkle with Parmesan cheese.

makes 2 servings

preparation time: 20 minutes

Crispy Italian Herb Chicken with
Tri-Color Rotini Pasta

Speedy Spaghetti with Sausage

    12 ounces whole wheat spaghetti
     8 ounces hot Italian turkey sausage
     1 cup chopped onion
     3 cloves garlic, minced
     1 can (28 ounces) crushed or puréed tomatoes, undrained
     1 can (14½ ounces) no-salt-added stewed tomatoes, undrained
     1 teaspoon dried basil leaves
    ¼ teaspoon red pepper flakes (optional)
     1 large *or* 2 medium zucchini or yellow squash, cut into chunks
    ¼ cup grated Parmesan cheese

1. Cook spaghetti according to package directions. Drain and set aside.

2. Meanwhile, crumble sausage into large saucepan, discarding casings. Add onion and garlic. Cook over medium heat until sausage is no longer pink, stirring occasionally; drain if needed.

3. Add crushed tomatoes with juice, stewed tomatoes with juice, basil and pepper flakes; bring to a simmer. Stir in zucchini; return to a simmer and cook uncovered 15 minutes or until zucchini is tender and sauce thickens, stirring occasionally.

4. Top cooked pasta with meat sauce; sprinkle with cheese.   *makes 6 servings*

Speedy Spaghetti with Sausage

Fettuccine Romano Aldana

6 ounces plain fettuccine, cooked and drained
6 ounces spinach fettuccine, cooked and drained
¾ cup butter, divided
8 ounces mushrooms, sliced
⅔ cup chopped green onions with tops
2½ cups heavy cream, divided
1½ cups (6 ounces) grated Wisconsin Romano cheese, divided
¼ teaspoon ground nutmeg
⅓ pound prosciutto ham slices, julienned
White pepper

Melt ¼ cup butter in large skillet over medium-high heat. Add mushrooms and onions; cook and stir until tender. Remove from skillet; set aside. Add remaining ½ cup butter to skillet; heat until lightly browned. Add 1 cup cream; bring to a boil. Reduce heat to low; simmer until slightly thickened, about 5 minutes. Add pasta, 1 cup cream, 1 cup cheese and nutmeg; mix lightly. Combine remaining ½ cup cream and cheese with mushroom mixture and prosciutto. Pour over hot pasta mixture; toss lightly. Season with pepper to taste.

makes 4 to 6 servings

Favorite recipe from **Wisconsin Milk Marketing Board**

Easy Lasagna

1 pound lean ground beef
1 jar (28 ounces) meatless spaghetti sauce
16 ounces cottage cheese
8 ounces sour cream
8 uncooked lasagna noodles
3 packages (6 ounces each) sliced mozzarella cheese (12 slices)
½ cup grated Parmesan cheese
1 cup water

continued on page 121

1. For meat sauce, cook beef in large skillet over medium-high heat until meat is brown, stirring to separate meat; drain. Add spaghetti sauce. Reduce heat to low. Heat through, stirring occasionally; set aside.

2. Preheat oven to 350°F.

3. Combine cottage cheese and sour cream in medium bowl; blend well.

4. Spoon 1½ cups of meat sauce in 13×9-inch baking dish. Layer with 4 uncooked noodles, ½ of cheese mixture, 4 slices mozzarella cheese, ½ of remaining meat sauce and ¼ cup Parmesan cheese. Repeat layers starting with uncooked noodles. Top with remaining 4 slices mozzarella cheese. Pour water around sides of dish. Cover tightly with foil.

5. Bake lasagna 1 hour. Uncover; bake 20 minutes more or until bubbly. Let stand 15 to 20 minutes before cutting. Garnish as desired. Serve immediately.   *makes 8 to 10 servings*

Pasta, Chicken & Broccoli Pesto Toss

4 ounces (about 2 cups) uncooked vegetable spiral pasta
2 cups cubed, cooked chicken or turkey breast meat
2 cups small broccoli florets, cooked crisp-tender, cooled
1½ cups (6 ounces) SARGENTO® Light Mozzarella Shredded Cheese
⅔ cup lightly packed fresh basil leaves
2 cloves garlic
1 cup mayonnaise
1 tablespoon lemon juice
½ teaspoon salt
½ cup (1½ ounces) SARGENTO® Fancy Parmesan Shredded Cheese
½ cup pine nuts or coarsely chopped walnuts, toasted

Cook pasta according to package directions until tender; drain and cool. Combine pasta, chicken, broccoli and Mozzarella cheese in large bowl. Blend basil and garlic in covered blender or food processor until finely chopped. Add mayonnaise, lemon juice and salt. Process to combine thoroughly. Stir in Parmesan cheese. Add to pasta mixture; toss to coat well. Stir in pine nuts. Serve immediately or cover and refrigerate. For maximum flavor, remove from refrigerator and toss gently 30 minutes before serving.   *makes 8 servings*

Rigatoni

2 pounds BOB EVANS® Italian Dinner Link Sausage
2 medium onions, sliced
3 green bell peppers, sliced
3 red bell peppers, sliced
3 cloves garlic, minced
1 tablespoon sugar
1 teaspoon dried oregano leaves
1 teaspoon dried basil leaves
1 teaspoon dried thyme leaves
   Salt and black pepper to taste
1 (1-quart) can crushed Italian plum tomatoes, undrained
1 pound rigatoni pasta, cooked according to package directions and drained
   Chopped fresh parsley (optional)

Cut sausage into 1-inch pieces. Cook in large saucepan over medium-high heat until well browned. Remove sausage to paper towels; set aside. Drain off all but ¼ cup drippings. Add all remaining ingredients except tomatoes, pasta and parsley to drippings. Cook and stir until vegetables are tender. Stir in reserved sausage and tomatoes with juice. Bring to a boil. Reduce heat to low; simmer 15 minutes. Serve over hot pasta. Garnish with chopped parsley, if desired. Refrigerate leftovers.   *makes 8 to 10 servings*

Rigatoni

Tuna and Broccoli Fettuccine

4 cups broccoli flowerets
½ pound fettuccine noodles
1 cup (8 ounces) part skim ricotta cheese
½ cup low fat milk
⅓ cup grated Parmesan cheese
½ teaspoon garlic salt
½ teaspoon Italian herb seasoning
Salt and pepper to taste
1 can (12 ounces) STARKIST® Solid White or Chunk Light Tuna, drained and chunked

In large saucepan of boiling water, cook broccoli until crisp-tender. Remove with slotted spoon to serving bowl. In same saucepan, cook fettuccine; drain, rinse and add to broccoli. In same saucepan, combine remaining ingredients except tuna; mix well. Heat thoroughly, stirring frequently, until sauce is smooth and thick. Add tuna. Pour over fettuccine and broccoli; toss gently.   *makes 5 servings*

Chicken with Roasted Garlic Marinara

1 package (9 ounces) DI GIORNO® Angel's Hair
1 package (6 ounces) LOUIS RICH® Italian Style or Grilled Chicken Breast Strips
1 package (10 ounces) DI GIORNO® Roasted Garlic Marinara Sauce
DI GIORNO® Shredded Parmesan Cheese

PREPARE pasta as directed on package; drain.

MIX chicken breast strips and sauce in saucepan. Cook on medium heat 5 minutes or until thoroughly heated.

SERVE over pasta; sprinkle with cheese.   *makes 3 to 4 servings*

prep: 10 minutes
cook: 5 minutes

Tuna and Broccoli Fettuccine

Prego® Easy Spaghetti & Meatballs

1 pound ground beef
2 tablespoons water
⅓ cup seasoned dry bread crumbs
1 egg, beaten
1 jar (28 ounces) PREGO® Traditional Pasta Sauce *or* Pasta Sauce Flavored with
   Meat
4 cups hot cooked spaghetti

1. Mix beef, water, bread crumbs and egg. Shape meat mixture into 12 (2-inch) meatballs. Arrange in 2-quart shallow microwave-safe baking dish.

2. Microwave on HIGH 5 minutes or until meatballs are no longer pink (160°F). Pour off fat. Pour pasta sauce over meatballs. Cover and microwave 3 minutes more or until sauce is hot. Serve over spaghetti.   *makes 4 servings*

prep time: 15 minutes
cook time: 10 minutes

Prego® Zesty Ziti

1 pound Italian sausage, cut into ½-inch pieces
1 large onion, chopped (about 1 cup)
1 medium green pepper, diced (about 1 cup)
1 jar (28 ounces) PREGO® Three Cheese Pasta Sauce
4½ cups hot cooked medium tube-shaped macaroni

1. In medium skillet over medium heat, cook sausage, onion and pepper until sausage is no longer pink. Pour off fat.

2. Add pasta sauce. Heat to a boil. Serve over macaroni. Top with grated Parmesan cheese.
                                          makes 4 servings

prep time: 10 minutes
cook time: 20 minutes

Top to bottom: Prego® Zesty Ziti and
Prego® Easy Spaghetti & Meatballs

PORK, BEEF & VEAL

Italian Porketta

2 to 4 pounds boneless pork roast
3 tablespoons dill seed
1 tablespoon fennel seed
¼ teaspoon oregano
1 teaspoon lemon pepper
¼ teaspoon onion powder
¼ teaspoon garlic powder

Combine seasonings together and coat roast with mixture. Roast in a shallow pan at 325°F. for 45 minutes to 1 hour, until meat thermometer registers 155° to160°F. Let roast rest 5 to 10 minutes before carving.

makes 8 servings

preparation time: 5 minutes
cooking time: 60 minutes

Favorite recipe from **National Pork Producers Council**

Italian Porketta

Sausage, Peppers & Onions with Grilled Polenta

    5 cups canned chicken broth
1½ cups Italian polenta or yellow cornmeal
1½ cups cooked fresh corn or thawed frozen corn
    2 tablespoons butter or margarine
    1 cup (4 ounces) freshly grated Parmesan cheese
    6 Italian-style sausages
    2 small or medium red onions, sliced into rounds
    1 each medium red and green bell peppers, seeded and cut into 1-inch strips
   ½ cup Marsala or sweet vermouth (optional)
     Olive oil

To make polenta, bring chicken broth to a boil in large pot. Add polenta and cook at a gentle boil, stirring frequently, about 30 minutes. If polenta starts to stick and burn bottom of pot, add up to ½ cup water. During last 5 minutes of cooking, stir in corn and butter. Remove from heat; stir in Parmesan cheese. Transfer polenta to greased 13×9-inch baking pan; let cool until firm and set enough to cut. (Polenta can be prepared a day ahead and held in refrigerator.)

Prick each sausage in 4 or 5 places with fork. Place sausages, red onions and bell peppers in large shallow glass dish or large heavy plastic food storage bag. Pour Marsala over sausage and vegetables; cover dish or close bag. Marinate in refrigerator up to 4 hours, turning sausages and vegetables several times.

Oil hot grid to help prevent sticking. Cut polenta into squares, then cut into triangles, if desired. Brush one side with oil. Grill polenta, oiled side down, on a covered grill over medium KINGSFORD® Briquets about 4 minutes until lightly toasted. Halfway through grilling time, brush top with oil, then turn and continue grilling. Move polenta to edge of grill to keep warm.

When coals are medium-low, drain sausage and vegetables; discard wine. Grill sausage on covered grill 15 to 20 minutes until cooked through, turning several times. After sausage has cooked 10 minutes, place vegetables in center of grid. Grill vegetables 10 to 12 minutes until tender, turning once or twice. *makes 6 servings*

Sausage, Peppers & Onions with Grilled Polenta

Italian Pork Cutlets

          1 teaspoon CRISCO® Oil*
          6 (4 ounces each) lean, boneless center-cut pork loin slices, ¾ inch thick
          1 can (8 ounces) tomato sauce
      1½ cups sliced fresh mushrooms
          1 small green bell pepper, cut into strips
       ½ cup sliced green onions with tops
          1 teaspoon Italian seasoning
       ½ teaspoon salt
       ⅛ teaspoon black pepper
       ¼ cup water
          1 teaspoon cornstarch
       ½ cup (2 ounces) shredded low moisture part-skim mozzarella cheese
      2⅔ cups hot cooked rice (cooked without salt or fat)

Use your favorite Crisco Oil product.

1. Heat oil in large skillet on medium heat. Add meat. Cook until browned on both sides.

2. Add tomato sauce, mushrooms, bell pepper, onions, Italian seasoning, salt and black pepper. Reduce heat to low. Cover. Simmer 30 minutes or until meat is tender.

3. Combine water and cornstarch in small bowl. Stir until well blended. Add to juices in skillet. Cook and stir until thickened.

4. Sprinkle cheese over meat mixture. Cover. Heat until cheese melts. Serve with rice.

makes 6 servings

Italian Pork Cutlet

Sausage Vegetable Frittata

    5 eggs
¼ cup milk
    2 tablespoons grated Parmesan cheese
½ teaspoon dried oregano leaves
½ teaspoon black pepper
    1 (10-ounce) package BOB EVANS® Skinless Link Sausage
    2 tablespoons butter or margarine
    1 small zucchini, sliced (about 1 cup)
½ cup shredded carrots
⅓ cup sliced green onions with tops
¾ cup (3 ounces) shredded Swiss cheese
    Carrot curls (optional)

Whisk eggs in medium bowl; stir in milk, Parmesan cheese, oregano and pepper. Set aside. Cook sausage in large skillet over medium heat until browned, turning occasionally. Drain off any drippings. Remove sausage from skillet and cut into ½-inch lengths. Melt butter in same skillet. Add zucchini, shredded carrots and onions; cook and stir over medium heat until tender. Top with sausage, then Swiss cheese. Pour egg mixture over vegetable mixture. Stir gently to combine. Cook, without stirring, over low heat 8 to 10 minutes or until center is almost set. Remove from heat. Let stand 5 minutes before cutting into wedges; serve hot. Garnish with carrot curls, if desired. Refrigerate leftovers.   *makes 4 to 6 servings*

Tip

A frittata is an Italian omelet in which the eggs are combined with other ingredients, such as meat, vegetables and herbs. The egg mixture is cooked in a heavy skillet slowly over low heat. The top of the frittata may be finished either by turning over the omelet or by placing it under the broiler. The frittata is then cut into wedges and served.

Sausage Vegetable Frittata

Pork Medallions with Marsala

1 pound pork tenderloin, cut into ½-inch slices
  All-purpose flour
2 tablespoons olive oil
1 clove garlic, minced
½ cup sweet Marsala wine
2 tablespoons chopped fresh parsley

1. Lightly dust pork with flour. Heat oil in large skillet over medium-high heat until hot. Add pork slices; cook 3 minutes per side or until browned. Remove from pan. Reduce heat to medium.

2. Add garlic to skillet; cook and stir 1 minute. Add wine and pork; cook 3 minutes or until pork is barely pink in center. Remove pork from skillet. Stir in parsley. Simmer wine mixture until slightly thickened, 2 to 3 minutes. Serve over pork.   *makes 4 servings*

tip: For a special touch, sprinkle with chopped red onion just before serving.

prep/cook time: 20 minutes

Tip

Marsala is rich smoky-flavored wine imported from the Mediterranean island of Sicily. This sweet varietal is served with dessert or used for cooking. Dry Marsala is served as a before-dinner drink.

Pork Medallions with Marsala

Tuscan Pork with Peppers

    1 pound boneless pork chops, cut into 1-inch cubes
    1 medium onion, peeled and chopped
    2 cloves garlic, minced
    1 teaspoon olive oil
    1 (14½-ounce) can Italian-style tomatoes, undrained
    ½ cup dry white wine
    1 sweet red bell pepper, seeded and sliced
    1 green pepper, seeded and sliced

In large nonstick skillet over medium-high heat, sauté pork cubes, onion and garlic in oil until pork starts to brown, about 4 to 5 minutes. Add remaining ingredients, lower heat to a simmer. Cover and cook gently for 12 to 15 minutes. Taste for seasoning, adding salt and black pepper if desired. Serve with hot cooked rigatoni or penne, if desired.

makes 4 servings

preparation time: 30 minutes

Favorite recipe from **National Pork Producers Council**

Italian Sausage and Bell Pepper Pizza

    1 cup (½ of 15 ounce can) CONTADINA® Original Pizza Sauce
    1 (12-inch) prepared, pre-baked pizza crust
    1 cup (4 ounces) shredded mozzarella cheese, divided
    ½ cup (2 ounces) shredded Parmesan cheese
    4 ounces (about 2 links) mild Italian sausage, cooked and sliced or crumbled
    1 small green bell pepper, cut into thin strips

1. Spread pizza sauce onto crust to within 1 inch of edge.

2. Sprinkle with ½ cup mozzarella cheese, Parmesan cheese, sausage, bell pepper and remaining mozzarella cheese.

3. Bake according to pizza crust package directions or until crust is crisp and cheese is melted.

makes 8 servings

Italian Pork Skillet

1 pound pork tenderloin
1 small eggplant
1 medium summer squash
2 tablespoons olive oil, divided
1½ teaspoons salt, divided
⅛ teaspoon black pepper
1 clove garlic, minced
1 medium onion, thinly sliced
1 small red bell pepper, cut into thin strips
1 teaspoon Italian seasoning
⅓ cup water
1 teaspoon cornstarch

Partially freeze tenderloin. Cut pork diagonally into ¼-inch thick slices; quarter slices. Cut squash lengthwise in half. Place on flat sides and cut crosswise into ¼-inch-thick slices. Cut eggplant in half; cube halves. In skillet, brown half of pork in 1 tablespoon hot olive oil, stirring constantly; remove from pan. Add remaining pork; cook, stirring constantly until pork is browned. Sprinkle ¾ teaspoon salt and pepper over pork. Place remaining 1 tablespoon olive oil, eggplant and minced garlic in skillet and cook over medium-high heat 3 minutes. Add squash, onion, bell pepper, Italian seasoning and remaining ¾ teaspoon salt; cook 7 minutes, stirring occasionally. Combine water and cornstarch; stir into vegetables. Return pork to skillet and cook 3 to 4 minutes or until thickened, stirring occasionally.

makes 4 servings

preparation time: 20 minutes

Favorite recipe from **National Pork Producers Council**

Tuscan-Style Sausage Sandwiches

1 pound hot or sweet Italian sausage links, sliced
1 box (10 ounces) frozen chopped spinach, thawed and squeezed dry
1 small onion, sliced
½ cup fresh or drained canned sliced mushrooms
1 jar (26 to 28 ounces) RAGÚ® Hearty Robusto! Pasta Sauce
1 loaf Italian or French bread (about 16 inches long), cut into 4 rolls

In 12-inch skillet, brown sausage over medium-high heat. Stir in spinach, onion and mushrooms. Cook, stirring occasionally, 5 minutes or until sausage is done. Stir in Ragú® Hearty Robusto! Pasta Sauce; heat through.

For each sandwich, split open each roll and evenly spoon in sausage mixture. Sprinkle, if desired, with crushed red pepper flakes.   *makes 4 servings*

Quick and Easy Italian Sandwich

1 tablespoon olive or vegetable oil
½ pound mild Italian sausage, casing removed, sliced ½ inch thick
1 can (14.5 ounces) CONTADINA® Recipe Ready Tomatoes with Italian Herbs, undrained
½ cup sliced green bell pepper
6 sandwich-size English muffins, split, toasted
¼ cup (1 ounce) shredded Parmesan cheese, divided

1. Heat oil in medium skillet. Add sausage; cook 3 to 4 minutes or until no longer pink in center, stirring occasionally. Drain.

2. Add undrained tomatoes and bell pepper; simmer, uncovered, 5 minutes, stirring occasionally.

3. Spread ½ cup meat mixture on each of 6 muffin halves; sprinkle with Parmesan cheese. Top with remaining muffin halves.   *makes 6 servings*

Tuscan-Style Sausage Sandwich

Grilled Pork and Potatoes Vesuvio

    1 center-cut boneless pork loin roast (1½ pounds), cut into 1-inch cubes
    ½ cup dry white wine
    2 tablespoons olive oil
    4 cloves garlic, minced and divided
1½ to 2 pounds small red potatoes (about 1½ inches in diameter), scrubbed
    6 lemon wedges
      Salt
      Pepper
    ¼ cup chopped fresh Italian or curly leaf parsley
    1 teaspoon finely grated lemon peel

1. Place pork in large resealable plastic food storage bag. Combine wine, oil and 3 cloves garlic in small bowl; pour over pork.

2. Place potatoes in single layer in microwavable dish. Pierce each potato with tip of sharp knife. Microwave at HIGH 6 to 7 minutes or until almost tender when pierced with fork. (Or, place potatoes in large saucepan. Cover with cold water. Bring to a boil over high heat. Simmer about 12 minutes or until almost tender when pierced with fork.) Immediately rinse with cold water; drain. Add to pork in bag. Seal bag, turning to coat. Marinate in refrigerator at least 2 hours or up to 8 hours, turning occasionally.

3. Prepare barbecue grill for direct cooking.

4. Meanwhile, drain pork mixture; discard marinade. Alternately thread about 3 pork cubes and 2 potatoes onto each of 6 skewers. Place 1 lemon wedge on end of each skewer. Season pork and potatoes to taste with salt and pepper.

5. Place skewers on grid. Grill skewers, on covered grill, over medium coals 14 to 16 minutes or until pork is juicy and no longer pink in center and potatoes are tender, turning halfway through grilling time.

6. Remove skewers from grill. Combine parsley, lemon peel and remaining minced garlic clove in small bowl. Sprinkle over pork and potatoes. To serve, squeeze lemon wedges over pork and potatoes. *makes 6 servings*

Grilled Pork and Potatoes Vesuvio

Lasagna Beef 'n' Spinach Roll-Ups

1½ pounds ground beef
1 (28-ounce) jar spaghetti sauce
½ cup A.1.® Original or A.1.® BOLD & SPICY Steak Sauce
½ teaspoon dried basil leaves
1 (15-ounce) container ricotta cheese
1 (10-ounce) package frozen chopped spinach, thawed, well drained
2 cups shredded mozzarella cheese (8 ounces)
⅓ cup grated Parmesan cheese, divided
1 egg, beaten
12 lasagna noodles, cooked, drained
2 tablespoons chopped fresh parsley

In large skillet, over medium-high heat, brown beef until no longer pink, stirring occasionally to break up beef; drain. In small bowl, mix spaghetti sauce, steak sauce and basil; stir 1 cup spaghetti sauce mixture into beef. Set aside remaining sauce mixture.

In medium bowl, mix ricotta cheese, spinach, mozzarella cheese, 3 tablespoons Parmesan cheese and egg. On each lasagna noodle, spread about ¼ cup ricotta mixture. Top with about ⅓ cup beef mixture. Roll up each noodle from short end; lay each roll, seam side down, in lightly greased 13×9×2-inch baking dish. Pour reserved spaghetti sauce mixture over noodles. Sprinkle with remaining Parmesan cheese and parsley. Bake, covered, at 350°F 30 minutes. Uncover and bake 15 to 20 minutes more or until hot and bubbly. Serve with additional Parmesan cheese if desired. Garnish as desired. *makes 6 servings*

Tip

To remove the excess moisture from frozen spinach, place it in a sieve and press it with the back of a spoon or squeeze the spinach in your hands.

Lasagna Beef 'n' Spinach Roll-Ups

Ragú® Steak Pizzaiola

4 eye-round steaks (1½ pounds)
2 tablespoons finely chopped garlic
4 tablespoons grated Parmesan cheese
½ teaspoon salt
½ teaspoon ground black pepper
2 cups frozen French-cut green beans, thawed
1 jar (26 to 28 ounces) RAGÚ® Hearty Robusto! Pasta Sauce

Preheat oven to 400°F. In bottom of 13×9-inch baking pan, arrange steaks; sprinkle with garlic, 2 tablespoons of the Parmesan cheese, salt and pepper. Add green beans and Ragú® Hearty Robust Blend Pasta Sauce. Bake 20 minutes or until desired doneness. Sprinkle with remaining cheese. Serve, if desired, over hot cooked noodles.   *makes 4 servings*

Cheesy Beef Stromboli

¾ pound lean ground beef
1 jar (16 ounces) RAGÚ® Cheese Creations!® Double Cheddar Sauce
1 teaspoon chili powder
1 pound frozen pizza or bread dough, thawed
1 egg yolk

1. Preheat oven to 375°F. In 10-inch skillet, brown ground beef over medium-high heat; drain. Remove from heat. Stir in ½ cup Ragú Cheese Creations! Sauce and chili powder and set aside.

2. Meanwhile, on greased jelly-roll pan, press dough to form 11×8-inch rectangle. Arrange beef mixture over dough, leaving 1-inch border around edges. Roll, starting at longest side, jelly-roll style. Fold in ends and pinch to seal. Arrange on pan, seam side down.

3. Brush with egg yolk. Bake 40 minutes or until bread is golden. Let stand 10 minutes before slicing. Serve with remaining sauce, heated.   *makes 6 servings*

prep time: 10 minutes
cook time: 40 minutes

Tip

A stromboli sandwich is made by wrapping pizza dough around a filling of meat and cheese, then baking it. Similar to a calzone, it was popularized in Philadelphia.

Roasted Herb & Garlic Tenderloin

1 well-trimmed beef tenderloin roast (3 to 4 pounds)
1 tablespoon black peppercorns
2 tablespoons chopped fresh basil *or* 2 teaspoons dried basil leaves
4½ teaspoons chopped fresh thyme *or* 1½ teaspoons dried thyme leaves
1 tablespoon chopped fresh rosemary *or* 1 teaspoon dried rosemary
1 tablespoon minced garlic
Salt and black pepper (optional)

1. Preheat oven to 425°F. To hold shape of roast, tie roast with cotton string in 1½-inch intervals.

2. Place peppercorns in small heavy resealable plastic food storage bag. Squeeze out excess air; seal bag tightly. Pound peppercorns with flat side of meat mallet or rolling pin until peppercorns are cracked.

3. Place roast on meat rack in shallow roasting pan. Combine cracked peppercorns, basil, thyme, rosemary and garlic in small bowl; rub over top surface of roast.

4. Roast in oven 40 to 50 minutes for medium or until internal temperatures reaches 145°F when tested with meat thermometer inserted into the thickest part of roast.

5. Transfer roast to cutting board; cover with foil. Let stand 10 to 15 minutes before carving. Internal temperature will continue to rise 5° to 10°F during stand time. Remove and discard string. To serve, carve crosswise into ½-inch-thick slices with large carving knife. Season with salt and pepper.

makes 10 to 12 servings

Tip

Fresh herbs contribute a livelier flavor to foods than dried herbs do. Look for them in the produce section of the supermarket. Or, grow your favorites in pots or your summer garden.

Roasted Herb & Garlic Tenderloin

Zesty Italian Stuffed Peppers

    3 bell peppers (green, red or yellow)
    1 pound ground beef
    1 jar (14 ounces) spaghetti sauce
  1⅓ cups *French's® Taste Toppers™* French Fried Onions, divided
    2 tablespoons *Frank's® RedHot®* Sauce
    ½ cup uncooked instant rice
    ¼ cup sliced ripe olives
    1 cup (4 ounces) shredded mozzarella cheese

Preheat oven to 400°F. Cut bell peppers in half lengthwise through stems; discard seeds. Place pepper halves, cut side up, in 2-quart shallow baking dish; set aside.

Place beef in large microwavable bowl. Microwave on HIGH 5 minutes or until meat is browned, stirring once. Drain. Stir in spaghetti sauce, ⅔ *cup* **Taste Toppers**, **RedHot** Sauce, rice and olives. Spoon evenly into bell pepper halves.

Cover; bake 35 minutes or until bell peppers are tender. Uncover; sprinkle with cheese and remaining ⅔ *cup* **Taste Toppers**. Bake 1 minute or until **Taste Toppers** are golden.

makes 6 servings

prep time: 10 minutes
cook time: 36 minutes

Zesty Italian Stuffed Pepper

Cheeseburger Calzones

1 pound ground beef
1 medium onion, chopped
½ teaspoon salt
1 jar (26 to 28 ounces) RAGÚ® Hearty Robusto!™ Pasta Sauce
1 jar (8 ounces) marinated mushrooms, drained and chopped (optional)
1 cup shredded Cheddar cheese (about 4 ounces)
1 package (2 pounds) frozen pizza dough, thawed

1. Preheat oven to 375°F. In 12-inch skillet, brown ground beef with onion and salt over medium-high heat; drain. Stir in 1 cup Ragú Pasta Sauce, mushrooms and cheese.

2. On floured board, cut each pound of dough into 4 pieces; press to form 6-inch circles. Spread ½ cup beef mixture on each dough circle; fold over and pinch edges to close.

3. With large spatula, gently arrange on cookie sheets. Bake 25 minutes or until golden. Serve with remaining sauce, heated.   *makes 8 servings*

prep time: 15 minutes
cook time: 25 minutes

Tip

This triangular or half-moon-shaped pizza turnover originated in Naples, where it is sold as street food. The pizza-dough crust encases fillings such as beef or sausage, vegetables and tomato sauce. It is almost always baked although it can be deep-fried.

Veal Parmigiana

    4 veal cutlets, cut ⅜ inch thick (about 4 ounces each)
    1 egg
    ¼ cup all-purpose flour
    ⅔ cup fine dry bread crumbs
    3 tablespoons olive oil, divided
    2 tablespoons butter
    1½ cups (6 ounces) shredded mozzarella cheese
    1 jar (28 ounces) pasta sauce with bell pepper
    ⅔ cup freshly grated Parmesan cheese
    Fresh basil leaves (optional)
    Hot cooked pasta

1. Pound veal with meat mallet to ¼-inch thickness. Pat dry with paper towels; set aside.

2. Beat egg in shallow bowl; spread flour and bread crumbs on separate plates. Dip reserved veal cutlets first in flour, then in egg, then in bread crumbs to coat both sides evenly. Press crumb coating firmly onto veal.

3. Heat 2 tablespoons oil and butter in large skillet over medium-high heat. Add veal. Cook 3 minutes per side or until browned.

4. Preheat oven to 350°F.

5. Remove veal with slotted spatula to ungreased 13×9-inch baking dish. Sprinkle mozzarella cheese evenly over veal. Spoon pasta sauce evenly over cheese. Sprinkle Parmesan cheese over tomato sauce. Drizzle remaining 1 tablespoon oil over top. Bake, uncovered, 25 minutes or until veal is tender and cheese is golden. Garnish with fresh basil, if desired. Serve with pasta.   *makes 4 servings*

Osso Buco

      3 pounds veal shanks (about 4 shanks)
 ¾ teaspoon salt, divided
 ½ teaspoon black pepper
 ½ cup all-purpose flour
      2 tablespoons olive oil
      1 cup chopped onion
      1 cup finely chopped carrot
      1 cup finely chopped celery
      2 cloves garlic, minced
 ½ cup dry white wine
      1 can (14½ ounces) diced tomatoes, undrained
      1 cup beef broth
      1 tablespoon chopped fresh basil or rosemary leaves
      1 bay leaf
      Parmesan Gremolata (recipe page 156)

1. Season veal shanks with ½ teaspoon salt and pepper. Place flour in shallow bowl; dredge veal shanks, one at a time, in flour, shaking off excess.

2. Heat oil in large ovenproof Dutch oven over medium-high heat until hot. Brown veal shanks 20 minutes, turning ¼ turn every 5 minutes and holding with tongs to brown all edges. Remove to plate.

3. Preheat oven to 350°F. Add onion, carrot, celery and garlic to Dutch oven; cook 5 minutes or until vegetables are soft. Pour wine over onion mixture. Cook over medium-high heat 2 to 3 minutes, stirring to scrape up any browned bits.

4. Add tomatoes with liquid, broth, basil, bay leaf and remaining ¼ teaspoon salt to Dutch oven; bring to a boil. Return veal shanks to Dutch oven; cover and bake 2 hours.

5. Meanwhile, prepare Parmesan Gremolata.

6. Discard bay leaf. Remove veal shanks to individual bowls; top with vegetable mixture. Sprinkle with Parmesan Gremolata.

makes 4 to 6 servings

continued on page 156

Osso Buco

Parmesan Gremolata

1 lemon
⅓ cup freshly grated Parmesan cheese
¼ cup chopped fresh parsley
1 clove garlic, minced

Finely grate lemon peel removing only yellow portion not white pith. Combine lemon peel, cheese, parsley and garlic. Cover; refrigerate. *makes about ⅓ cup*

Classic Veal Florentine

6 ounces fresh spinach, chopped
4 tablespoons butter or margarine, divided
2 cups marinara sauce
¼ teaspoon salt
⅛ teaspoon black pepper
¼ cup all-purpose flour
4 veal cutlets, cut ⅜ inch thick (about 4 ounces each)
1 tablespoon olive oil
1 cup (4 ounces) shredded mozzarella cheese

1. Place spinach in large saucepan over medium heat. Cover and steam 4 minutes or until tender, stirring occasionally. Add 2 tablespoons butter; cook and stir until butter is absorbed. Remove from pan; set aside.

2. Mix flour, salt and pepper in plastic resealable bag. Pound veal with meat mallet to ¼-inch thickness. Pat dry with paper towels. Shake veal, 1 cutlet at a time, in seasoned flour.

3. Heat oil and remaining 2 tablespoons butter in large skillet over medium heat until bubbly. Add veal; cook 2 to 3 minutes per side until light brown. Remove from heat. Spoon off excess fat. Top veal with reserved spinach, then cheese.

4. Pour marinara sauce into skillet, lifting edges of veal to let sauce flow under. Cook over low heat until bubbly. Cover and simmer 8 minutes or until heated through. Serve with pasta. Garnish as desired. *makes 4 servings*

Classic Veal Florentine

Veal Scallopini

4 veal cutlets, cut ⅜ inch thick (about 4 ounces each)
¼ cup butter or margarine
½ pound fresh mushrooms, thinly sliced
2 tablespoons olive oil
1 small onion, finely chopped
¼ cup dry sherry
2 teaspoons all-purpose flour
½ cup beef broth
¼ teaspoon salt
⅛ teaspoon black pepper
2 tablespoons heavy or whipping cream
Fresh bay leaf and marjoram sprigs for garnish
Hot cooked pasta (optional)

1. Place each veal cutlet between sheets of waxed paper on cutting board. Pound veal with meat mallet to ¼-inch thickness. Pat dry with paper towels; set aside.

2. Heat butter in large skillet over medium heat until melted and bubbly. Cook and stir mushrooms in hot butter 3 to 4 minutes until light brown. Remove mushrooms with slotted spoon to small bowl; set aside.

3. Add oil to butter remaining in skillet; heat over medium heat. Add veal; cook 2 to 3 minutes per side until light brown. Remove veal with slotted spatula to plate; set aside.

4. Add onion to same skillet; cook and stir 2 to 3 minutes until soft. Stir sherry into onion mixture. Bring to a boil over medium-high heat; boil 15 seconds. Stir in flour; cook and stir 30 seconds. Remove from heat; stir in broth. Bring to a boil over medium heat, stirring constantly. Stir in reserved mushrooms, salt and pepper. Add reserved veal to sauce mixture; reduce heat to low. Cover and simmer 8 minutes or until veal is tender. Remove from heat.

5. Push veal to one side of skillet. Stir cream into sauce mixture; mix well. Cook over low heat until heated through. Garnish, if desired. Serve immediately with pasta.

makes 4 servings

Veal Scallopini

CHICKEN & TURKEY

Chicken Tuscany

　6 medium red potatoes, scrubbed and sliced ⅛ inch thick
12 ounces shiitake, cremini, chanterelle and/or button mushrooms, sliced
　4 tablespoons olive oil, divided
　4 tablespoons grated Parmesan cheese, divided
　3 teaspoons minced garlic, divided
　3 teaspoons minced fresh rosemary or 1½ teaspoons dried rosemary leaves, divided
　　Salt and ground pepper
　1 package (about 3 pounds) PERDUE® fresh skinless Pick of the Chicken

Preheat oven to 425°F. Pat potatoes dry with paper towels. Toss potatoes and mushrooms with 2½ tablespoons oil, 2 tablespoons cheese, 2 teaspoons garlic, 2 teaspoons rosemary, ½ teaspoon salt and ¼ teaspoon pepper. In 13×9-inch baking dish, arrange potatoes in one layer; top with remaining 2 tablespoons cheese. Bake 15 minutes or until potatoes are lightly browned; set aside.

Meanwhile, in large nonstick skillet over medium heat, heat remaining 1½ tablespoons oil. Add chicken pieces. Season lightly with salt and pepper; sprinkle with remaining rosemary and garlic. Cook chicken 5 to 6 minutes on each side or until browned. (Do not crowd pan; if necessary, brown chicken in two batches.)

Arrange chicken on top of potato mixture; drizzle with any oil from skillet and return to oven. Bake 20 to 25 minutes longer or until chicken is no longer pink in center. Serve chicken, potatoes and mushrooms with green salad, if desired.　　　*makes 6 servings*

Chicken Tuscany

160

Skillet Chicken Cacciatore

2 tablespoons olive or vegetable oil
1 cup sliced red onion
1 medium green bell pepper, cut into strips (about 1 cup)
2 cloves garlic, minced
1 pound (about 4) boneless, skinless chicken breast halves
1 can (14.5 ounces) CONTADINA® Recipe Ready Diced Tomatoes with Italian
    Herbs, undrained
¼ cup dry white wine or chicken broth
½ teaspoon salt
¼ teaspoon ground black pepper
1 tablespoon chopped fresh basil *or* 1 teaspoon dried basil leaves, crushed

1. Heat oil in large skillet over medium-high heat. Add onion, bell pepper and garlic; sauté 1 minute.

2. Add chicken; cook 6 to 8 minutes or until chicken is no longer pink in center.

3. Add undrained tomatoes, wine, salt and black pepper. Simmer, uncovered, 5 minutes. Serve over hot cooked rice or pasta, if desired. Sprinkle with basil. *makes 6 servings*

Skillet Chicken Cacciatore

Classic Chicken Piccata

  4 boneless skinless chicken breast halves
  ¼ cup all-purpose flour
  1 egg, beaten
  ½ cup bread crumbs
  1 teaspoon dried parsley flakes
  ¼ teaspoon salt
  ¼ teaspoon freshly ground black pepper
  3 tablespoons olive oil
  ⅓ cup dry white wine
  ¼ cup fresh lemon juice
    Lemon slices, for garnish

1. Place chicken between 2 pieces of plastic wrap; pound to ½-inch thickness. Place flour on small plate. Place egg in shallow bowl. Combine bread crumbs, parsley, salt and pepper on another small plate. Roll each breast half in flour, then in egg. Coat with bread crumb mixture.

2. Heat oil in medium nonstick skillet over medium-high heat. Add chicken; cook 4 minutes. Turn; reduce heat to medium. Cook 4 to 5 minutes or until chicken is no longer pink in center. Transfer chicken to serving platter; keep warm. Add wine and lemon juice to skillet; cook and stir over high heat 2 minutes. Spoon sauce over chicken. Garnish with lemon slices, if desired.   *makes 4 servings*

Tip

It is best to use a good table wine for cooking; choose one that you enjoy drinking. It doesn't need to be a fine wine. Avoid products labeled as cooking wines because they contain salt. You may substitute broth or water if wine isn't available but the flavor of the dish will be less complex.

Classic Chicken Piccata

Chicken Breasts Smothered in Tomatoes and Mozzarella

4 boneless skinless chicken breast halves (about 1½ pounds)
3 tablespoons olive oil, divided
1 cup chopped onions
2 teaspoons bottled minced garlic
1 can (14 ounces) Italian-style stewed tomatoes
1½ cups (6 ounces) shredded mozzarella cheese

1. Preheat broiler.

2. Pound chicken breasts between 2 pieces of plastic wrap to ¼-inch thickness using flat side of meat mallet or rolling pin.

3. Heat 2 tablespoons oil in ovenproof skillet over medium heat. Add chicken; cook about 3½ minutes per side or until no longer pink in center. Transfer to plate; cover and keep warm.

4. Heat remaining 1 tablespoon oil in same skillet over medium heat. Add onions and garlic; cook and stir 3 minutes. Add tomatoes; bring to a simmer. Return chicken to skillet, spooning onion and tomato mixture over chicken.

5. Sprinkle cheese over top. Broil 4 to 5 inches from heat until cheese is melted.

makes 4 servings

prep and cook time: 20 minutes

Tip

Mozzarella is a soft white cheese that melts easily. In southern Italy, where it originated, it is made from the milk of buffaloes. In other parts of Italy and in North America, it is made from cow's milk. Choose part-skim mozzarella for less fat and calories.

Chicken Breast Smothered in Tomatoes and Mozzarella

Chicken Marsala

4 BUTTERBALL® Boneless Skinless Chicken Breast Fillets
3 cups sliced fresh mushrooms
2 tablespoons sliced green onion
2 tablespoons water
¼ teaspoon salt
¼ cup dry Marsala wine
1 teaspoon cornstarch

Flatten chicken fillets between two pieces of plastic wrap. Spray nonstick skillet with nonstick cooking spray; heat over medium heat until hot. Add chicken; cook 2 to 3 minutes on each side or until no longer pink in center. Transfer to platter; keep warm. Add mushrooms, onion, water and salt to skillet. Cook 3 minutes or until most of the liquid has evaporated. Combine wine and cornstarch in small bowl; add to skillet. Heat, stirring constantly, until thickened. Spoon over warm chicken. *makes 4 servings*

preparation time: 15 to 20 minutes

Chicken Marsala

Chicaboli

      4 boneless, skinless chicken breast halves
    ¼ teaspoon salt
      4 slices deli ham
    12 slices pepperoni
      4 thin slices provolone cheese
        Prepared mustard
      2 eggs, beaten
      1 cup fine dry bread crumbs
    ½ cup CRISCO® Oil*
        Buttered linguini
        Marinara sauce (optional)

Use your favorite Crisco Oil product.

Rinse chicken; pat dry. Sprinkle with salt. Top each with ham, 3 slices pepperoni, cheese and 2 small dots mustard. Fold chicken so that all meat and cheese are enclosed. (Secure with toothpicks, if desired.) Dip in eggs. Roll in crumbs.

Heat oven to 375°F.

Heat oil in medium skillet on medium high heat. Add chicken. Brown lightly on all sides. Transfer to 13×9×2-inch glass baking dish.

Bake for 25 minutes or until chicken is no longer pink in center. *Do not overbake.* Remove toothpicks. Serve with linguini. Top with marinara sauce, if desired.   *makes 4 servings*

Tip

Provolone is a firm Italian cheese with a mild, smoky flavor. If it is unavailable, you may substitute mozzarella cheese.

Chicken with Escarole and Eggplant

4 bone-in chicken breast halves (about 1½ pounds)
2 tablespoons olive or vegetable oil
1 tablespoon chopped garlic
1 large head escarole, chopped
1 small eggplant (about 1 pound), peeled and cubed
1 jar (26 to 28 ounces) RAGÚ® Hearty Robusto!™ Pasta Sauce

1. Preheat oven to 450°F. Season chicken, if desired, with salt and pepper. In bottom of broiler pan without rack, arrange chicken. Roast 40 minutes or until chicken is no longer pink in center.

2. Meanwhile, in 12-inch skillet, heat oil over medium heat and cook garlic, stirring occasionally, 30 seconds. Add escarole and eggplant and cook covered, stirring occasionally, 5 minutes, or until escarole is wilted. Stir in Ragú Pasta Sauce and cook 10 minutes or until vegetables are tender.

3. With slotted spoon, remove vegetables to large serving platter, then top with chicken. Serve, if desired, over hot cooked pasta or rice. *makes 4 servings*

prep time: 10 minutes
cook time: 40 minutes

Tip

Escarole is a pale green leafy vegetable with a slightly bitter flavor. It is often added to salad green mixtures. Escarole's crispy firm leaves are sturdy enough to stand up to sautéing and make a flavorful addition to Italian soups or main dishes.

Chicken with Tomato-Basil Cream Sauce

4 boneless, skinless chicken breast halves (about 1¼ pounds), pounded, if desired
3 tablespoons I CAN'T BELIEVE IT'S NOT BUTTER!® Spread, divided
2 plum tomatoes, chopped
1 small onion, chopped
¼ teaspoon salt
¼ cup dry white wine or chicken broth
½ cup whipping or heavy cream
2 tablespoons loosely packed fresh basil leaves, cut in thin strips

Season chicken, if desired, with salt and ground black pepper.

In 12-inch nonstick skillet, melt 2 tablespoons I Can't Believe It's Not Butter! Spread over medium-high heat and cook chicken 8 minutes or until chicken is no longer pink, turning once. Remove chicken and set aside.

In same skillet, melt remaining 1 tablespoon I Can't Believe It's Not Butter! Spread and cook tomatoes, onion and salt, stirring occasionally, 3 minutes or until tomatoes are tender. Stir in wine and cook, stirring occasionally, 2 minutes or until wine evaporates. Stir in cream. Reduce heat to low and return chicken to skillet. Simmer uncovered 4 minutes or until sauce is thickened and chicken is heated through. Garnish with basil.   *makes 4 servings*

Tip

Fresh basil tends to bruise and discolor easily. To avoid this, stack the leaves together and roll them up cigar style. With a sharp knife, cut the leaves crosswise into strips.

Chicken with Tomato-Basil Cream Sauce

Fresco Marinated Chicken

    1 envelope LIPTON® RECIPE SECRETS® Garlic Mushroom Soup Mix*
    ⅓ cup water
    ¼ cup olive or vegetable oil
    1 teaspoon lemon juice or vinegar
    4 boneless, skinless chicken breast halves (about 1¼ pounds)

Also terrific with LIPTON® RECIPE SECRETS® Savory Herb with Garlic or Golden Onion Soup Mix.

1. For marinade, blend all ingredients except chicken.

2. In shallow baking dish or plastic bag, pour ½ cup of the marinade over chicken. Cover, or close bag, and marinate in refrigerator, turning occasionally, up to 3 hours. Refrigerate remaining marinade.

3. Remove chicken, discarding marinade. Grill or broil chicken, turning once and brushing with refrigerated marinade until chicken is no longer pink.   *makes 4 servings*

Little Italy Chicken and Rice

    1 package (about 4 pounds) PERDUE® Fresh Pick of the Chicken
    1 teaspoon dried Italian herb seasoning
      Salt and ground pepper to taste
    2 tablespoons olive oil
    1 cup uncooked white rice
    1 large onion, coarsely chopped
    1 green bell pepper, seeded and diced
    1 can (14½ ounces) Italian-style stewed tomatoes
    2 cups chicken broth

Season chicken with Italian seasoning, salt and pepper. Preheat oven to 375°F. In ovenproof Dutch oven over medium-high heat, heat oil. Add chicken; cook 6 to 8 minutes until brown on all sides, turning occasionally. Remove and set aside.

To drippings in pan, add rice, onion and bell pepper; sauté 2 to 3 minutes. Return chicken to Dutch oven; stir in tomatoes and chicken broth. Cover and bake in oven 45 to 50 minutes until rice is tender and chicken is cooked through.   *makes 5 to 6 servings*

Fresco Marinated Chicken

Chicken Primavera

2 tablespoons CRISCO® Oil*
6 boneless, skinless chicken breast halves, cut into 1-inch pieces (about
    1½ pounds chicken)
1 clove garlic, minced
3 cups broccoli flowerets
2 cups sliced fresh mushrooms
1 fresh tomato, chopped
1 package (8 ounces) spaghetti or linguine, cooked and well drained
¾ cup grated Parmesan cheese
1 tablespoon dried basil leaves
½ teaspoon salt
¼ teaspoon pepper
¾ cup evaporated skimmed milk

Use your favorite Crisco Oil product.

1. Heat oil in large skillet on medium-high heat. Add chicken and garlic. Cook and stir 5 minutes or until chicken is no longer pink in center. Remove to serving plate.

2. Add broccoli, mushrooms and tomato to skillet. Cook and stir 3 to 5 minutes or until broccoli is crisp-tender. Return chicken to skillet to heat. Transfer mixture to large serving bowl. Add spaghetti, Parmesan cheese, basil, salt and pepper. Toss to mix. Add milk. Mix lightly. Serve immediately on spinach-covered plates, if desired. *makes 6 servings*

Chicken Primavera

Chicken Rolls Stuffed with Peppers

    4 boneless skinless chicken breast halves (about 1¼ pounds)
    1 cup water
    ½ teaspoon onion powder
    ¼ teaspoon garlic powder
    2 cups thin red, yellow and/or green bell pepper strips
    1½ teaspoons olive oil, divided
    ¼ teaspoon dried oregano leaves
    ¼ teaspoon dried thyme leaves
    ⅛ teaspoon black pepper
    1 tablespoon grated Romano cheese
    1 tablespoon fine dry bread crumbs

Preheat oven to 350°F. Pound chicken breasts between two sheets of waxed paper with flat side of meat mallet to about ¼-inch thickness. Store chicken in refrigerator until needed.

Combine water, onion powder and garlic powder in small saucepan; bring to a boil over high heat. Add bell peppers; return to a boil. Reduce heat to medium-low. Simmer, covered, 2 to 3 minutes or until bell peppers are crisp-tender. Drain.

Combine ½ teaspoon oil, oregano, thyme and black pepper in small bowl. Spread mixture over one side of flattened chicken breasts; arrange bell peppers on top. Roll up chicken; secure with wooden toothpicks or metal skewers. Place chicken, seam side down, in ungreased 8-inch square baking dish. Brush chicken with remaining 1 teaspoon oil.

Combine Romano cheese and bread crumbs in small cup; sprinkle over chicken. Bake, uncovered, 20 to 25 minutes or until chicken is golden brown and no longer pink in center. Remove toothpicks before serving.

makes 4 servings

Chicken Tuscany

1 (2½- to 3-pound) chicken, cut into serving pieces
1 medium red or green bell pepper, cut into strips
1 jar (4½ ounces) sliced mushrooms, drained
1 envelope LIPTON® RECIPE SECRETS® Onion Soup Mix
1 can (14½ ounces) whole peeled tomatoes, undrained and chopped
½ cup orange juice or water
2 tablespoons firmly packed brown sugar
1 tablespoons olive or vegetable oil (optional)

1. Preheat oven to 425°F. In 13×9-inch baking pan, arrange chicken, red bell pepper and mushrooms; set aside.

2. In medium bowl, combine remaining ingredients; pour over chicken.

3. Bake uncovered 50 minutes or until chicken is no longer pink.   *makes 4 servings*

recipe tip: It's easy to substitute your favorite bone-in chicken parts (all legs, breasts or thighs) for a whole cut-up chicken. Just be sure to substitute the same amount by weight.

Quickest Chicken Cacciatore

4 BUTTERBALL® Boneless Skinless Chicken Thighs
2 tablespoons butter or margarine
1 jar (14 ounces) chunky-style meatless spaghetti sauce
1 jar (2½ ounces) sliced mushrooms, drained
½ cup chopped green bell pepper
¼ cup dry red wine
1 package (9 ounces) refrigerated fettuccine, cooked and drained

Cut each chicken thigh lengthwise into 3 pieces. Melt butter in large skillet over medium heat. Add chicken; cook 8 to 10 minutes or until no longer pink in center. Add remaining ingredients except fettuccine. Cook and stir until heated through. Serve over fettuccine.

makes 4 servings

preparation time: 15 minutes

Simmered Tuscan Chicken

    2 tablespoons olive or vegetable oil
    1 pound boneless, skinless chicken breasts, cut into 1-inch cubes
    2 cloves garlic, finely chopped
    4 medium potatoes, cut into ½-inch cubes (about 4 cups)
    1 medium red bell pepper, cut into large pieces
    1 jar (26 to 28 ounces) RAGÚ® Old World Style® Pasta Sauce
    1 pound fresh or frozen cut green beans
    1 teaspoon dried basil leaves, crushed
       Salt and ground black pepper to taste

In 12-inch skillet, heat oil over medium-high heat and cook chicken with garlic until chicken is no longer pink. Remove chicken and set aside.

In same skillet, add potatoes and bell pepper. Cook over medium heat, stirring occasionally, 5 minutes. Stir in remaining ingredients. Bring to a boil over high heat. Reduce heat to low and simmer covered, stirring occasionally, 35 minutes or until potatoes are tender. Return chicken to skillet and heat through.   *makes 6 servings*

Ragu® Chicken Cacciatore

    1 tablespoon olive oil
    2 pounds boneless, skinless chicken thighs
    1 jar (26 to 28 ounces) RAGÚ® Old World Style Pasta Sauce—Traditional
    1 can (6 ounces) sliced mushrooms, drained
    ½ teaspoon dried thyme leaves, crushed (optional)

Season chicken, if desired, with salt and pepper. In 6-quart saucepan, heat oil over medium-high heat and brown chicken in two batches. Stir in Ragú® Old World Style Pasta Sauce, mushrooms and thyme. Bring to a boil over high heat. Reduce heat to low and simmer covered, stirring occasionally, 10 minutes or until chicken is no longer pink in center. Serve, if desired, over hot cooked pasta.   *makes 4 servings*

Simmered Tuscan Chicken

Chicken Scaloppine with Lemon-Caper Sauce

1 pound boneless skinless chicken breasts
3 tablespoons all-purpose flour, divided
¼ teaspoon black pepper
¼ teaspoon chili powder
½ cup fat-free, reduced-sodium chicken broth
1 tablespoon lemon juice
1 tablespoon drained capers
½ teaspoon olive oil

1. Place chicken breasts, 1 at a time, between sheets of waxed paper. Pound to ¼-inch thickness. Combine 2 tablespoons flour, pepper and chili powder in shallow plate. Dip chicken pieces in flour mixture to lightly coat both sides.

2. Combine broth, lemon juice, remaining flour and capers in small bowl.

3. Spray large skillet with nonstick cooking spray; heat over medium-high heat. Place chicken in hot pan in single layer; cook 1½ minutes. Turn over; cook 1 to 1½ minutes or until chicken is no longer pink in center. Repeat with remaining chicken (brush pan with ¼ teaspoon oil each time you add pieces to prevent sticking). If cooking more than 2 batches, reduce heat to medium to prevent burning chicken.

4. Stir broth mixture and pour into skillet. Boil 1 to 2 minutes or until thickened. Serve immediately over chicken.

makes 4 servings

Tip

Capers are the small, pea-sized bud of a flower from the caper bush. Found mostly in Central America and the Mediterranean, capers add pungency to sauces, dips and relishes. Usually these green buds are pickled and can be found in the condiment section of the supermarket. They taste very much like gherkin pickles.

Chicken Scaloppine with
Lemon-Caper Sauce

Chicken Rustigo

4 boneless skinless chicken breast halves
1 package (10 ounces) fresh mushrooms, sliced
¾ cup chicken broth
¼ cup dry red wine or water
3 tablespoons *French's*® Hearty Deli Brown Mustard
2 medium tomatoes, seeded and coarsely chopped
1 can (14 ounces) artichoke hearts, drained and quartered
2 teaspoons cornstarch

1. Season chicken with salt and pepper. Heat *1 tablespoon oil* in large nonstick skillet over medium-high heat. Cook chicken 5 minutes or until browned on both sides. Remove and set aside.

2. Heat *1 tablespoon oil* in same skillet until hot. Add mushrooms. Cook and stir 5 minutes or until mushrooms are tender. Stir in broth, wine and mustard. Return chicken to skillet. Add tomatoes and artichoke hearts. Heat to boiling. Reduce heat to medium-low. Cook, covered, 10 minutes or until chicken is no longer pink in center.

3. Combine cornstarch with *1 tablespoon cold water.* Stir into skillet. Heat to boiling. Cook, stirring, over high heat about 1 minute or until sauce thickens. Serve with hot cooked orzo pasta, if desired.   *makes 4 servings*

tip: To seed tomatoes, cut them in half crosswise. Gently squeeze tomato halves until seeds come out.

prep time: 10 minutes
cook time: 21 minutes

Chicken Rustigo

Chicken Florentine

  4 (6 ounces) skinless, boneless chicken breast halves
½ teaspoon salt
½ teaspoon freshly ground black pepper
½ cup Italian seasoned dry bread crumbs
 1 egg, separated
 1 (10-ounce) package frozen chopped spinach, thawed, well drained
⅛ teaspoon nutmeg
 2 tablespoons olive oil
 4 slices SARGENTO® Deli Style Sliced Mozzarella Cheese
 1 cup prepared tomato basil or marinara spaghetti sauce, heated

1. Sprinkle chicken with salt and pepper. Place bread crumbs in a shallow plate. Beat egg white in a shallow bowl. Dip each chicken breast in egg white, letting excess drip off, roll lightly in crumbs, patting to coat well. (At this point, chicken may be covered and refrigerated up to 4 hours before cooking.)

2. Combine spinach, egg yolk and nutmeg; mix well. Heat oil in a large skillet (with cover) over medium-high heat until hot. Add chicken breasts; cook 3 minutes per side or until golden brown. Reduce heat to low. Top each chicken breast with ¼ of spinach mixture and 1 slice of cheese. Cover skillet and continue cooking 6 minutes or until chicken is no longer pink in center. Spoon spaghetti sauce over chicken. *makes 4 servings*

preparation time: 15 minutes
cooking time: 12 minutes

Chicken Florentine

Chicken with Peppers, Zucchini and Tomatoes on Angel Hair

½ cup sun-dried tomatoes (not oil-packed)
3 tablespoons all-purpose flour
¼ teaspoon salt
¼ teaspoon ground red pepper
1 pound chicken tenders, cut into ¾-inch pieces
1 tablespoon olive oil
2 cloves garlic, minced
¼ cup dry vermouth
1 can (14½ ounces) diced Italian-style tomatoes
2 small zucchini, sliced
1 large red bell pepper, cut into thin strips
1 large yellow bell pepper, cut into thin strips
1 tablespoon fresh thyme leaves *or* 1 teaspoon dried thyme leaves
½ cup water
½ pound uncooked angel hair pasta

1. Place sun-dried tomatoes in small bowl; cover with boiling water. Let tomatoes soak for 5 to 10 minutes or until soft. Drain; cut into slivers.

2. Combine flour, salt and red pepper in medium bowl; mix well. Add chicken; toss until evenly coated. Heat olive oil in large nonstick skillet over medium-high heat. Add chicken; cook without stirring 3 to 4 minutes or until golden. Turn chicken; cook 3 minutes longer.

3. Add garlic; cook and stir 1 minute. Add vermouth; stir to loosen skillet drippings. Add canned tomatoes, dried tomatoes, zucchini, bell peppers, thyme and water; bring to a boil. Cover; reduce heat to low and simmer 5 minutes or until zucchini is tender, stirring occasionally. Set aside and keep warm.

4. Cook pasta according to package directions, omitting salt. Drain. Transfer to large serving bowl. Pour sauce over pasta; garnish with thyme sprigs, if desired. *makes 6 servings*

Prego® Quick Chicken Parmigiana

1 package (about 10 ounces) frozen fully cooked breaded chicken patties *or*
    1 package (about 14 ounces) refrigerated fully cooked breaded chicken cutlets
1 jar (28 ounces) PREGO® Traditional Pasta Sauce
2 tablespoons grated Parmesan cheese
½ cup shredded mozzarella cheese (2 ounces)
4 cups hot cooked spaghetti (about 8 ounces uncooked)

1. In 2-quart shallow baking dish arrange patties. Top each with ¼ *cup* pasta sauce. Sprinkle with Parmesan cheese and mozzarella cheese.

2. Bake at 400°F. for 15 minutes or until chicken is hot and cheese is melted.

3. Heat remaining sauce until hot. Serve sauce with chicken and spaghetti.

makes 4 servings

microwave directions: In 2-quart shallow microwave-safe baking dish arrange patties. Microwave on HIGH 4 minutes (3 minutes for refrigerated cutlets). Top each patty with ¼ *cup* pasta sauce, 1 *teaspoon* Parmesan cheese and 2 *tablespoons* mozzarella cheese. Microwave 2 minutes more or until sauce is hot and cheese is melted.

chicken nuggets parmigiana: Substitute 1 package (10 to 13 ounces) frozen *or* refrigerated fully cooked breaded chicken nuggets for chicken patties. In 2-quart shallow microwave-safe baking dish arrange nuggets. Microwave on HIGH 3½ minutes (2½ minutes for refrigerated). Pour pasta sauce evenly over nuggets. Top with cheeses. Microwave 2 minutes more or until sauce is hot and cheese is melted.

prep time: 5 minutes
cook time: 15 minutes

Italian Chicken Breasts

1 pound BOB EVANS® Italian Roll Sausage
1 cup sliced fresh mushrooms
1 clove garlic, minced
3 (8-ounce) cans tomato sauce
1 (6-ounce) can tomato paste
1½ teaspoons Italian seasoning
4 boneless, skinless chicken breast halves
1 cup (4 ounces) shredded mozzarella cheese
Hot cooked pasta

Preheat oven to 350°F. Crumble sausage into large skillet. Cook over medium heat until browned, stirring occasionally. Remove sausage; set aside. Add mushrooms and garlic to drippings; cook and stir until tender. Stir in reserved sausage, tomato sauce, tomato paste and seasoning. Bring to a boil. Reduce heat to low; simmer 15 minutes to blend flavors. Meanwhile, arrange chicken in greased 11×7-inch baking dish. Pour tomato sauce mixture over chicken; cover with foil. Bake 40 minutes; uncover. Sprinkle with cheese; bake 5 minutes more. Serve over pasta. Refrigerate leftovers. *makes 4 servings*

Italian Chicken Breasts

Chicken Cacciatore

8 ounces dry noodles
1 can (15 ounces) chunky Italian-style tomato sauce
1 cup chopped green bell pepper
1 cup sliced onion
1 cup sliced mushrooms
4 boneless skinless chicken breast halves (1 pound)

1. Cook noodles according to package directions; drain.

2. While noodles are cooking, combine tomato sauce, bell pepper, onion and mushrooms in microwavable dish. Cover loosely with plastic wrap or waxed paper; microwave at HIGH 6 to 8 minutes, stirring halfway through cooking time.

3. While sauce mixture is cooking, coat large skillet with nonstick cooking spray and heat over medium-high heat. Cook chicken breasts 3 to 4 minutes per side or until lightly browned.

4. Add sauce mixture to skillet with salt and pepper to taste. Reduce heat to medium and simmer 12 to 15 minutes. Serve over noodles. *makes 4 servings*

prep and cook time: 30 minutes

Chicken Cacciatore

Pollo alla Firènze

2 cups plus 2 tablespoons dry sherry, divided
3 whole chicken breasts, split and boned
3 tablespoons olive oil
2 cloves garlic, minced
3 cups fresh spinach leaves, cut in thin shreds
2 cups coarsely chopped mushrooms
1 cup grated carrots
⅓ cup sliced green onions
Salt and pepper to taste
1½ cups prepared Italian salad dressing
1 cup Italian-seasoned dry bread crumbs
⅓ cup grated Romano cheese
Steamed fresh asparagus
Parsley sprigs and carrot strips for garnish

1. Pour 2 cups sherry into large, shallow dish. Add chicken, turning to coat. Cover; marinate in refrigerator 3 hours.

2. Heat oil in large skillet over medium heat. Add garlic, spinach, mushrooms, grated carrots, green onions, salt, pepper and remaining 2 tablespoons sherry. Cook and stir 3 to 5 minutes or until spinach is completely wilted; cool spinach mixture.

3. Place dressing in another shallow dish; set aside.

4. Combine bread crumbs with Romano cheese in third shallow dish; set aside.

5. Preheat oven to 375°F.

6. Remove chicken from marinade; discard marinade. Slice a pocket into side of each chicken breast where breasts were originally attached. Fill pockets in chicken with spinach mixture. Secure pockets with wooden toothpicks to enclose mixture.

7. Coat each filled chicken breast with dressing, shaking off excess. Place each chicken breast in bread crumb mixture; spoon bread crumb mixture over chicken to coat.

8. Place chicken in single layer in greased 13×9-inch baking pan. Drizzle with remaining dressing. Cover; bake 15 minutes. Uncover; bake 10 minutes or until chicken is tender. Remove toothpicks. Serve with asparagus. Garnish, if desired. *makes 6 servings*

Pollo alla Firènze

Turkey Scaloppine

    1 pound turkey cutlets or 4 boneless, skinless chicken breast halves (about
        1 pound)
    2 tablespoons all-purpose flour
 1½ teaspoons LAWRY'S® Seasoned Salt, divided
    1 teaspoon LAWRY'S® Lemon Pepper
    3 tablespoons olive oil, divided
    1 medium-sized green bell pepper, cut into strips
    1 cup sliced butternut squash or zucchini
  ½ cup sliced fresh mushrooms
    1 teaspoon cornstarch
  ½ teaspoon LAWRY'S® Garlic Powder with Parsley
  ¼ cup dry white wine
  ⅓ cup chicken broth
    1 tablespoon plus 1½ teaspoons lemon juice

Place turkey between two sheets of waxed paper; pound to ⅛-inch thickness. In large resealable plastic food storage bag, combine flour, ¾ teaspoon Seasoned Salt and Lemon Pepper. Add turkey, a few pieces at a time, to plastic bag; seal bag. Shake until well coated. In large skillet, heat 2 tablespoons oil; add turkey and cook about 5 minutes on each side or until no longer pink in center. Remove from skillet; keep warm. In same skillet, heat remaining 1 tablespoon oil. Add bell pepper, squash and mushrooms; cook until bell peppers are crisp-tender. Reduce heat to low. In small bowl, combine cornstarch, Garlic Powder with Parsley and remaining ¾ teaspoon Seasoned Salt; mix well. Stir in combined wine, broth and lemon juice. Add to skillet. Bring just to a boil over medium-high heat, stirring constantly. Simmer 1 minute. Garnish, if desired.   *makes 4 servings*

serving suggestion: On platter, layer vegetables, turkey or chicken and top with sauce.

Turkey Scaloppine

Butterball® Sweet Italian Sausage with Vesuvio Potatoes

1 package BUTTERBALL® Lean Fresh Turkey Sweet Italian Sausage
4 baking potatoes, cut lengthwise into wedges
2 tablespoons olive oil
½ teaspoon coarse ground black pepper
1 can (14½ ounces) chicken broth
6 cloves garlic, minced
½ cup dry white wine
6 tablespoons minced fresh parsley
2 tablespoons grated Parmesan cheese
Salt

Grill sausage according to package directions. Combine potatoes, oil and pepper in large bowl. Spray large nonstick skillet with nonstick cooking spray; add potato mixture. Cook 15 minutes. Add chicken broth and garlic; cook, covered, 10 minutes or until potatoes are tender. Add wine and parsley; cook, uncovered, 5 minutes. Sprinkle with Parmesan cheese. Add salt to taste. Serve with grilled sausage.   *makes 6 servings*

preparation time: 30 minutes

Cutlets Milanese

1 package (about 1 pound) PERDUE® FIT 'N EASY® Fresh Thin-Sliced Turkey or Chicken Breast Cutlets
Salt and ground pepper to taste
½ cup Italian seasoned bread crumbs
½ cup grated Parmesan cheese
1 large egg beaten with 1 teaspoon water
2 to 3 tablespoons olive oil

Season cutlets with salt and pepper. On wax paper, combine bread crumbs and Parmesan cheese. Dip cutlets in egg mixture and roll in bread crumb mixture. In large, nonstick skillet over medium-high heat, heat oil. Add cutlets and sauté 3 minutes per side, until golden brown and cooked through.   *makes 4 servings*

Polenta with Turkey and Mushrooms

1 pound assorted fresh mushrooms (combination of shiitake, crimini and button
    mushrooms), sliced
1 tablespoon fresh tarragon, minced
1 teaspoon salt, divided
¼ teaspoon black pepper
3 tablespoons olive oil
2 cups cubed cooked Turkey
2 cups milk, divided
1 cup yellow cornmeal
½ cup grated Parmesan cheese
    Fresh tarragon sprigs for garnish

1. In 12-inch skillet over medium-high heat, sauté mushrooms, minced tarragon, ½ teaspoon salt and pepper in hot oil until mushrooms are golden brown, about 10 minutes.

2. Add turkey and ⅓ cup water, stirring to loosen all browned bits from bottom of skillet. Keep warm.

3. Meanwhile, in 3-quart saucepan, place 1⅓ cups milk and remaining ½ teaspoon salt; gradually whisk in cornmeal until smooth. In 2-quart saucepan, heat remaining ⅔ cup milk and 2 cups water to boiling over high heat; whisk into cornmeal mixture. Heat to boiling over medium-high heat, whisking. Reduce heat to low. Cook while stirring, 5 minutes or until thick. Stir in Parmesan cheese.

4. Serve polenta topped with turkey-mushroom mixture. Garnish with fresh tarragon sprigs.

makes 8 appetizer or 4 main-dish servings

Favorite recipe from **National Turkey Federation**

Tip

Polenta, an important part of Northern Italian cuisine, is made from cornmeal. It is prepared by cooking cornmeal and water together to a thick spoonable consistency. It is served as a hot cereal or side dish with butter and sometimes Parmesan cheese. Here it is served with a turkey and mushroom mixture.

Turkey Piccata

⅓ cup all-purpose flour
½ teaspoon salt
½ teaspoon black pepper
1 boneless turkey breast (1 pound), sliced into 4 slices
3 tablespoons olive oil, divided
1½ cups sliced fresh mushrooms
2 cloves garlic, crushed
½ cup chicken broth
2 tablespoons lemon juice
½ teaspoon dried oregano leaves
3 tablespoons pine nuts
2 tablespoons chopped fresh parsley

1. Combine flour, salt and pepper in resealable plastic food storage bag. Add turkey; shake to evenly coat with flour mixture. Set aside.

2. Heat 2 tablespoons oil in large skillet over medium-high heat until hot. Add turkey; cook 3 minutes on each side or until lightly browned and turkey is no longer pink in center. Remove from skillet to serving plate. Cover with foil and keep warm.

3. Add remaining 1 tablespoon oil to skillet. Heat over medium-high heat until hot. Add mushrooms and garlic. Cook and stir 2 minutes. Add broth, lemon juice and oregano. Bring to a boil. Reduce heat to medium; simmer, uncovered, 3 minutes.

4. Spoon sauce mixture over turkey. Sprinkle with pine nuts and parsley. Serve immediately.

makes 4 servings

serving suggestion: Serve with rice pilaf, sliced fresh tomatoes, garlic bread and caramel sundaes.

prep and cook time: 20 minutes

Turkey Piccata

FISH & SHELLFISH

Shrimp Scampi

2 tablespoons olive or vegetable oil
½ cup diced onion
1 large clove garlic, minced
1 small green bell pepper, cut into strips
1 small yellow bell pepper, cut into strips
8 ounces medium shrimp, peeled, deveined
1 can (14.5 ounces) CONTADINA® Recipe Ready Diced Tomatoes with Italian
    Herbs, undrained
2 tablespoons chopped fresh parsley *or* 2 teaspoons dried parsley flakes
1 tablespoon lemon juice
½ teaspoon salt

1. Heat oil in large skillet over medium-high heat. Add onion and garlic; sauté 1 minute.

2. Add bell peppers; sauté 2 minutes. Add shrimp; cook 2 minutes or until shrimp turn pink.

3. Add undrained tomatoes, parsley, lemon juice and salt; cook 2 to 3 minutes or until heated through. Serve over hot cooked pasta, if desired. *makes 4 servings*

Shrimp Scampi

Angel Hair Pasta with Seafood Sauce

½ pound firm whitefish, such as sea bass, monkfish or grouper
2 teaspoons olive oil
½ cup chopped onion
2 cloves garlic, minced
3 pounds fresh plum tomatoes, seeded and chopped
¼ cup chopped fresh basil
2 tablespoons chopped fresh oregano
1 teaspoon crushed red pepper
½ teaspoon sugar
2 bay leaves
½ pound fresh bay scallops or shucked oysters
8 ounces uncooked angel hair pasta
2 tablespoons chopped fresh parsley

1. Cut whitefish into ¾-inch pieces. Set aside.

2. Heat oil in large nonstick skillet over medium heat; add onion and garlic. Cook and stir 3 minutes or until onion is tender. Reduce heat to low; add tomatoes, basil, oregano, crushed red pepper, sugar and bay leaves. Cook, uncovered, 15 minutes, stirring occasionally.

3. Add whitefish and scallops. Cook, uncovered, 3 to 4 minutes or until fish flakes easily when tested with fork and scallops are opaque. Remove bay leaves; discard. Set seafood sauce aside.

4. Cook pasta according to package directions. Drain well. Combine pasta with seafood sauce in large serving bowl. Mix well. Sprinkle with parsley.   *makes 6 servings*

Tip

There are two common varieties of scallops. Tiny bay scallops tend to cost more than sea scallops, which are about three times as large. If cut into halves or thirds, sea scallops make an economical alternative to bay scallops.

Angel Hair Pasta with Seafood Sauce

Red Snapper Scampi

¼ cup margarine or butter, softened
1 tablespoon white wine
1½ teaspoons minced garlic
½ teaspoon grated lemon peel
⅛ teaspoon black pepper
1½ pounds red snapper, orange roughy or grouper fillets (about 4 to 5 ounces each)

1. Preheat oven to 450°F. Combine margarine, wine, garlic, lemon peel and pepper in small bowl; stir to blend.

2. Place fish on foil-lined shallow baking pan. Top with seasoned margarine. Bake 10 to 12 minutes or until fish begins to flake easily when tested with fork.   *makes 4 servings*

serving suggestion: Serve fish over mixed greens. Or, add sliced carrots, zucchini and bell pepper cut into matchstick-size strips to the baking pan for an easy vegetable side dish.

prep and cook time: 12 minutes

Tip

Red snapper, orange roughy and grouper are all lean, firm fish with a mild flavor. The skin of grouper has a very strong flavor; always remove it before cooking.

Red Snapper Scampi

Red Clam Sauce with Vegetables

2 cups sliced fresh mushrooms
1 can (14½ ounces) no-salt-added stewed tomatoes, undrained
1 cup chopped green bell pepper
1 can (8 ounces) no-salt-added tomato sauce
½ cup chopped onion
1½ teaspoons dried basil leaves
¾ teaspoon dried savory leaves
½ teaspoon black pepper
1 small yellow squash, sliced and halved
2 cans (6½ ounces each) minced clams, drained, reserving liquid
2 tablespoons cornstarch
3 cups hot cooked spaghetti

Combine mushrooms, tomatoes with juice, bell pepper, tomato sauce, onion, basil, savory and black pepper in large saucepan. Bring to a boil over medium-high heat. Reduce heat to medium. Cover and cook 5 to 6 minutes or until vegetables are tender.

Stir in squash and clams. Combine ½ cup clam liquid and cornstarch in small bowl. Stir into mixture in saucepan. Cook and stir over medium heat until mixture boils and thickens. Cook and stir 2 minutes more. Serve over spaghetti. *makes 4 servings*

Red Clam Sauce with Vegetables

Milano Shrimp Fettucine

4 ounces egg or spinach fettucine
½ pound medium shrimp, peeled and deveined
1 clove garlic, minced
1 tablespoon olive oil
1 can (14½ ounces) DEL MONTE® Pasta Style Chunky Tomatoes
½ cup whipping cream
¼ cup sliced green onions

1. Cook pasta according to package directions; drain.

2. Cook shrimp and garlic in hot oil in large skillet over medium-high heat until shrimp are pink and opaque.

3. Stir in tomatoes; simmer 5 minutes. Blend in cream and green onions; heat through. *Do not boil.* Serve over hot pasta.   *makes 3 to 4 servings*

prep & cook time: 20 minutes

Tip

To devein shrimp, cut a shallow slit along the back of the shrimp with a paring knife. Lift out the vein. (You may find this easier to do under cold running water.) The veins of large and jumbo shrimp are gritty; they must always be removed. The veins of medium and small shrimp are not gritty and need not be removed unless you want a more elegant presentation.

Scampi Italienne

½ pound uncooked shrimp, peeled and deveined
¼ cup *plus* 1 tablespoon CRISCO® Oil*, divided
3 tablespoons dry white wine
½ teaspoon grated lemon peel
1 tablespoon lemon juice
½ teaspoon dried basil leaves
½ teaspoon dried oregano leaves
1 clove garlic, minced
¼ teaspoon salt
⅛ teaspoon pepper
2 drops hot pepper sauce
¾ cup uncooked rice
1½ cups water
2 tomatoes, cut into ½-inch pieces
¼ cup chopped fresh parsley
2 green onions with tops, sliced

*Use your favorite Crisco Oil product.

1. Place shrimp in medium glass or stainless steel bowl.

2. Combine ¼ cup oil, wine, lemon peel, lemon juice, basil, oregano, garlic, salt, pepper and hot pepper sauce in container with tight-fitting lid. Shake well. Remove 1 tablespoon oil mixture. Reserve. Pour remaining oil mixture over shrimp. Turn to coat. Refrigerate 30 minutes, turning once.

3. Heat reserved 1 tablespoon marinade in medium saucepan on medium-high heat. Add rice. Stir 1 minute. Pour water over rice. Stir. Bring to a boil. Reduce heat to low. Cover. Simmer 15 to 20 minutes or until tender. Remove from heat. Fluff with fork. Stir in tomatoes. Cover.

4. Heat remaining 1 tablespoon oil in large skillet on high heat. Drain shrimp. Add to skillet. Stir-fry 1 minute or until shrimp turn pink.

5. Spoon rice mixture onto serving platter. Pour shrimp mixture over rice. Sprinkle with parsley and green onions. Season with additional salt and pepper, if desired.

makes 4 servings

Seafood Risotto

1 package (5.2 ounces) rice in creamy sauce (Risotto Milanese flavor)
1 package (14 to 16 ounces) frozen fully cooked shrimp
1 box (10 ounces) BIRDS EYE® frozen Mixed Vegetables
2 teaspoons grated Parmesan cheese

• In 4-quart saucepan, prepare rice according to package directions. Add frozen shrimp and vegetables during last 10 minutes of cooking.

• Sprinkle with cheese.   *makes 4 servings*

serving suggestion: Serve with garlic bread and a tossed green salad.

prep time: 5 minutes
cook time: 15 minutes

Campbell's® Seafood Tomato Alfredo

1 tablespoon margarine *or* butter
1 medium onion, chopped (about ½ cup)
1 can (10¾ ounces) CAMPBELL'S® Condensed Cream of Mushroom with Roasted Garlic Soup
½ cup milk
1 cup diced canned tomatoes
1 pound firm white fish (cod, haddock *or* halibut), cut into 2-inch pieces
4 cups hot cooked linguine (about 8 ounces uncooked)

1. In medium skillet over medium-high heat, heat margarine. Add onion and cook until tender.

2. Add soup, milk and tomatoes. Heat to a boil. Add fish. Reduce heat to low. Cook 10 minutes or until fish flakes easily when tested with a fork. Serve over linguine.

makes 4 servings

prep/cook time: 20 minutes

Seafood Risotto

Seafood Primavera

⅓ cup olive oil
1 medium onion, chopped
4 green onions with tops, chopped
3 cloves garlic, minced
3 carrots, cut into julienne strips
1 zucchini, cut into julienne strips
1 each small red and yellow bell pepper, cut into strips
3 ounces snow peas
⅓ cup sliced mushrooms
½ pound peeled and deveined medium shrimp
½ pound scallops
⅔ cup bottled clam juice
⅓ cup dry white wine
1 cup heavy cream
½ cup freshly grated Parmesan cheese
⅔ cup flaked crabmeat
2 tablespoons lemon juice
2 tablespoons chopped fresh parsley
¼ teaspoon dried basil
¼ teaspoon oregano leaves
    Black pepper to taste
1 package (8 ounces) linguine, cooked and drained

Heat oil in large skillet over medium-high heat. Add onions and garlic; cook and stir until tender. Add remaining vegetables. Reduce heat to medium-low; cover. Simmer until tender, stirring occasionally. Remove vegetable mixture from skillet; set aside.

Add shrimp and scallops to skillet; cook and stir until shrimp turn pink and scallops are opaque. Remove from skillet, reserving liquid in skillet. Add clam juice and wine to skillet; bring to a boil. Stir in cream and Parmesan cheese. Reduce heat; simmer 3 minutes until thickened, stirring constantly.

Return vegetables and seafood to skillet. Heat thoroughly, stirring occasionally. Stir in all remaining ingredients except linguine. Pour over hot linguine in large bowl; toss gently to coat.   *makes 6 servings*

Seafood Primavera

Linguine with White Clam Sauce

2 tablespoons CRISCO® Oil*
2 cloves garlic, minced
2 cans (6½ ounces *each*) chopped clams, undrained
½ cup chopped fresh parsley
¼ cup dry white wine or clam juice
1 teaspoon dried basil leaves
1 pound linguine, cooked (without salt or fat) and well drained

*Use your favorite Crisco Oil product.

1. Heat oil and garlic in medium skillet on medium heat.

2. Drain clams, reserving liquid. Add reserved liquid and parsley to skillet. Reduce heat to low. Simmer 3 minutes, stirring occasionally.

3. Add clams, wine and basil. Simmer 5 minutes, stirring occasionally. Add to hot linguine. Toss lightly to coat.   *makes 8 servings*

Poached Seafood Italiano

1 tablespoon olive or vegetable oil
1 large clove garlic, minced
¼ cup dry white wine or chicken broth
4 (6 ounces) salmon steaks or fillets
1 can (14.5 ounces) CONTADINA® Recipe Ready Diced Tomatoes with Italian
    Herbs, undrained
2 tablespoons chopped fresh basil (optional)

1. Heat oil in large skillet. Add garlic; sauté 30 seconds. Add wine. Bring to boil.

2. Add salmon; cover. Reduce heat to medium; simmer 6 minutes.

3. Add undrained tomatoes; simmer 2 minutes or until salmon flakes easily when tested with fork. Sprinkle with basil just before serving, if desired.   *makes 4 servings*

Poached Seafood Italiano

Spicy Shrimp Puttanesca

8 ounces uncooked linguine, capellini or spaghetti
1 tablespoon olive oil
12 ounces medium shrimp, peeled and deveined
4 cloves garlic, minced
¾ teaspoon red pepper flakes
1 cup finely chopped onion
1 can (14½ ounces) no-salt-added stewed tomatoes, undrained
2 tablespoons tomato paste
2 tablespoons chopped pitted kalamata or black olives
1 tablespoon drained capers
¼ cup chopped fresh basil or parsley

1. Cook linguine according to package directions, omitting salt. Drain; set aside.

2. Meanwhile, heat oil in large nonstick skillet over medium high heat. Add shrimp, garlic and red pepper flakes; cook and stir 3 to 4 minutes or until shrimp are opaque. Transfer shrimp mixture to bowl with slotted spoon; set aside.

3. Add onion to same skillet; cook over medium heat 5 minutes, stirring occasionally. Add tomatoes with juice, tomato paste, olives and capers; simmer, uncovered, 5 minutes.

4. Return shrimp mixture to skillet; simmer 1 minute. Stir in basil; simmer 1 minute. Place linguine in large serving bowl; top with shrimp mixture.   *makes 4 servings*

Tip

Kalamata olives are from Greece. They are almond-shaped with a dark purplish-black color. They are soaked in a wine vinegar marinade and have a rich, fruity flavor. These olives are generally sold unpitted.

Spicy Shrimp Puttanesca

Creamy Alfredo Seafood Lasagna

1 jar (16 ounces) RAGÚ® Cheese Creations!® Classic Alfredo Sauce
1 container (15 ounces) ricotta cheese
1 pound imitation crabmeat, separated into bite-sized pieces
1 green onion, chopped (optional)
¼ teaspoon ground white pepper
⅛ teaspoon ground nutmeg (optional)
9 lasagna noodles, cooked and drained
2 cups shredded mozzarella cheese (about 8 ounces)
2 tablespoons grated Parmesan cheese

1. Preheat oven to 350°F. In medium bowl, combine ½ cup Ragú Cheese Creations! Sauce, ricotta cheese, crabmeat, green onion, pepper and nutmeg; set aside.

2. In 13×9-inch baking dish, spread ½ cup Ragú Cheese Creations! Sauce. Arrange 3 lasagna noodles lengthwise over sauce. Spread ½ of the ricotta mixture over noodles; evenly top with ¾ cup mozzarella cheese. Repeat layers, ending with noodles. Top with remaining ½ cup sauce, then sprinkle with remaining ½ cup mozzarella cheese and Parmesan cheese.

3. Cover with aluminum foil and bake 40 minutes. Remove foil and continue baking 10 minutes or until cheese is melted and lightly golden. Let stand 10 minutes before serving. Garnish, if desired, with additional chopped green onions. *makes 8 servings*

prep time: 20 minutes
cook time: 50 minutes

Tip

Ricotta cheese resembles cottage cheese but is smoother, richer and drier. Like so many ingredients used in Italian cooking, it is inexpensive and readily available.

Grilled Shrimp Italiano

⅓ cup extra-virgin olive oil
¼ cup balsamic vinegar
1 envelope GOOD SEASONS® Italian Salad Dressing Mix
1 pound medium shrimp, cleaned
2 green bell peppers, cut into 1½-inch chunks
2 tablespoons chopped fresh basil

MIX olive oil, vinegar and salad dressing mix in cruet or small bowl as directed on envelope. Pour over shrimp in shallow dish; cover. Refrigerate several hours or overnight to marinate. Drain; discard marinade.

ARRANGE shrimp and green peppers alternately on skewers. Place on greased grill over hot coals.

GRILL 5 to 6 minutes on each side or until shrimp are pink. Sprinkle with basil.

makes 4 servings

prep: 10 minutes plus marinating
grill: 12 minutes

Tip

Balsamic vinegar is made from sweet white grapes. Because it is aged for many years to develop its characteristic mellow sweet flavor, it is expensive. Use it in small amounts to add flavor to salads and cooked dishes. Any wine vinegar can be substituted for it.

Linguine with Pesto-Marinara Clam Sauce

     1 teaspoon vegetable oil
     ¼ cup chopped shallots
     3 cloves garlic, finely chopped
     2 cans (6 ounces each) minced clams
 1⅓ cups Marinara Sauce (recipe follows)
     2 tablespoons prepared pesto sauce
     ¼ teaspoon crushed red pepper
     8 ounces uncooked linguine
     ¼ cup chopped fresh parsley

1. Heat oil in large nonstick saucepan over medium heat until hot. Add shallots and garlic. Cook, covered, 2 minutes.

2. Drain clams; reserve ½ cup juice. Add clams, reserved juice, Marinara Sauce, pesto and red pepper to saucepan. Cook 10 minutes, stirring often.

3. Prepare linguine according to package directions, omitting salt. Drain. Spoon sauce evenly over each serving; top with parsley. Garnish with lemon slices and additional parsley, if desired.

makes 4 servings

Marinara Sauce

 1½ tablespoon olive oil
     3 cloves garlic, minced
     1 can (28 ounces) Italian plum tomatoes, undrained
     ¼ cup tomato paste
     2 teaspoons dried basil leaves
     ½ teaspoon sugar
     ¼ teaspoon salt
     ¼ teaspoon red pepper flakes

Heat oil in large skillet over medium heat. Add garlic; cook and stir 3 minutes. Stir in remaining ingredients. Bring to a boil. Reduce heat to low; simmer, uncovered, 10 minutes.

makes about 3½ cups

Linguine with Pesto-Marinara Clam Sauce

Orzo Risotto with Shrimp and Vegetables

Nonstick cooking spray
1 zucchini, sliced and halved
2 teaspoons grated lemon peel
1 cup sliced mushrooms
½ cup chopped onion
2 cloves garlic
¾ teaspoon dried sage leaves
¼ to ½ teaspoon dried thyme leaves
1¼ cups uncooked orzo
2 cans (14½ ounces each) fat-free reduced-sodium chicken broth
8 ounces shrimp, peeled and deveined
¾ cup frozen peas, thawed
¼ cup grated Parmesan cheese
Salt and black pepper

1. Spray large saucepan with cooking spray. Heat over medium heat until hot. Add zucchini and lemon peel; cook and stir 2 to 3 minutes or until zucchini is tender. Remove from saucepan; set aside.

2. Add mushrooms, onion, garlic, sage and thyme to saucepan; cook and stir 2 to 3 minutes or until onion is tender. Stir in orzo; cook and stir until browned.

3. Bring chicken broth to a boil in medium saucepan. Add broth to orzo mixture, ½ cup at a time, stirring constantly until broth is absorbed before adding next ½ cup. Continue cooking 10 to 15 minutes or until orzo is tender.

4. Stir shrimp and peas into orzo mixture during last half of cooking time; stir in zucchini mixture last 2 to 3 minutes of cooking time. Stir in cheese; season to taste with salt and pepper.

makes 4 main-dish servings

Orzo Risotto with Shrimp and Vegetables

Baked Snapper with Artichokes

Juice of 2 lemons
3 large artichokes
8 tablespoons olive oil, divided
2 cloves garlic, minced
1 whole red snapper or sea bass (about 2 pounds), gutted and scaled with head and tail intact
Salt and black pepper to taste
3 small sprigs fresh rosemary, divided
1 tablespoon finely chopped fresh parsley

1. Pour half the lemon juice and squeezed lemon halves in large bowl. Fill bowl half full with cold water; set aside. Reserve remaining lemon juice.

2. To prepare artichokes, bend back dark outer leaves and snap off at base. Continue snapping off leaves until bottom halves of leaves are yellow. Cut $1\frac{1}{2}$ inches off tops of artichokes; trim stems to 1 inch. Peel tough green layer from stem and base. Cut artichokes lengthwise (from tops) into quarters; place quarters in lemon water to help prevent discoloration.

3. Working with 1 artichoke quarter at a time, remove small heart-shaped leaves from center by grasping with fingers, then pulling and twisting. Scoop out fuzzy choke with spoon.

4. Cut artichoke quarters lengthwise into thin slices. Quickly return slices to lemon water. Repeat step 3 with remaining artichoke quarters.

5. Drain artichoke slices. Heat 6 tablespoons oil in large skillet over medium heat until hot. Add artichokes and garlic. Cover; cook 5 minutes until tender, stirring occasionally.

6. Preheat oven to 425°F. Rinse fish; pat dry with paper towels. Season fish inside and out with salt and pepper. Place in baking pan.

7. Stuff fish with as many artichoke slices as will fit and 1 sprig rosemary. Arrange remaining artichoke slices and 2 sprigs rosemary around fish.

8. Combine reserved lemon juice, remaining 2 tablespoons oil and parsley; drizzle over fish. Bake 30 minutes or until fish flakes when tested with fork, basting occasionally with pan juices.

makes 4 servings

Baked Snapper with Artichokes

Fish alla Milanese

⅓ cup plus 2 tablespoons olive oil, divided
2 tablespoons lemon juice
½ teaspoon salt
   Dash pepper
1 small onion, finely chopped
1 pound flounder or haddock fillets (4 to 8 pieces)
2 eggs
1 tablespoon milk
½ cup all-purpose flour
¾ cup fine dry unseasoned bread crumbs
¼ cup plus 2 tablespoons butter or margarine, divided
1 clove garlic, minced
1 tablespoon chopped fresh parsley
   Fresh thyme sprig for garnish
   Lemon slices (optional)

1. For marinade, whisk ⅓ cup oil, lemon juice, salt and pepper in small bowl; stir in onion. Pour marinade into 13×9-inch glass baking dish.

2. Rinse fish; pat dry with paper towels. Place fish in baking dish; spoon marinade over fish to coat thoroughly. Marinate, covered, in refrigerator 1 hour, turning fish over occasionally.

3. Combine eggs and milk in shallow bowl; mix well. Spread flour and bread crumbs on separate plates. Remove fish from marinade; pat dry with paper towels. Discard marinade.

4. Dip fish to coat both sides evenly, first in flour, then in egg mixture, then in bread crumbs. Press crumb coating firmly onto fish. Place on waxed paper; refrigerate 15 minutes.

5. Heat remaining 2 tablespoons oil and 2 tablespoons butter in large nonstick skillet over medium heat until melted and bubbly; add fish. Cook 2 to 3 minutes per side until fish flakes easily with a fork and topping is light brown. Remove to heated serving plate.

6. Melt remaining ¼ cup butter in medium skillet over medium heat. Add garlic. Cook 1 to 2 minutes until butter turns light brown; stir in parsley. Pour browned butter mixture over fish. Garnish, if desired. Serve immediately with lemon slices. *makes 4 servings*

Fish alla Milanese

Zesty Shrimp and Pasta

1 pound large shrimp, cleaned
1 cup prepared GOOD SEASONS® Zesty Italian Salad Dressing for Fat Free
    Dressing, divided
2 cups sliced fresh mushrooms
1 small onion, thinly sliced
1 can (14 ounces) artichoke hearts, drained, cut into halves
1 tablespoon chopped fresh parsley
1 package (9 ounces) DI GIORNO® Pasta, any variety, cooked as directed on
    package, drained
¼ cup KRAFT® 100% Grated Parmesan Cheese

COOK and stir shrimp in ½ cup of the dressing in large skillet on medium-high heat
2 minutes.

ADD mushrooms, onion, artichoke hearts and parsley. Continue cooking until shrimp are
pink and vegetables are tender.

TOSS with hot cooked pasta and remaining ½ cup dressing. Sprinkle with cheese.

makes 6 servings

variation: For a sophisticated variation, prepare salad dressing mix with olive oil and
balsamic vinegar.

variation: Prepare as directed, substituting scallops for shrimp.

variation: Prepare as directed, substituting hot cooked MINUTE® White Rice for pasta.

prep: 10 minutes
cook: 15 minutes

Zesty Shrimp and Pasta

MEATLESS ENTRÉES

Fusilli with Fresh Red & Yellow Tomato Sauce

  ½ cup (1 stick) I CAN'T BELIEVE IT'S NOT BUTTER!® Spread
   1 medium onion, chopped
   2 cloves garlic, finely chopped (optional)
1½ pounds red and/or yellow cherry tomatoes, halved
  ⅓ cup chopped fresh basil leaves
   1 box (16 ounces) fusilli (long curly pasta) or linguine, cooked and drained
     Grated Parmesan cheese

In 12-inch nonstick skillet, melt I Can't Believe It's Not Butter! Spread over medium heat and cook onion, stirring occasionally, 2 minutes or until softened. Stir in garlic and tomatoes and cook, stirring occasionally, 5 minutes or until tomatoes soften but do not lose their shape and sauce thickens slightly. Stir in basil and season, if desired, with salt and ground black pepper.

In large serving bowl, toss sauce with hot fusilli and sprinkle with cheese.

makes 4 servings

Fusilli with Fresh Red & Yellow
Tomato Sauce

Polenta Squares with Chunky Tomato Sauce

2 tablespoons butter
½ cup chopped green bell pepper
½ cup chopped onion
2 cloves garlic, minced
4 cups milk
½ teaspoon salt
¼ teaspoon cayenne pepper
1 cup yellow cornmeal
½ cup grated Parmesan cheese
1 jar (28 ounces) prepared chunky garden vegetable-style spaghetti sauce
1½ cups (6 ounces) shredded provolone cheese

1. Melt butter in medium saucepan over medium heat. Add bell pepper, onion and garlic; cook and stir 5 minutes or until vegetables are tender. Remove from saucepan with slotted spoon; set aside.

2. Bring milk, salt and cayenne pepper to a boil in large, heavy saucepan over medium-high heat. While whisking milk mixture vigorously, add cornmeal in very thin but steady stream. *Do not let lumps form.* Reduce heat to low.

3. Cook, uncovered, 40 to 60 minutes until polenta is very thick, stirring frequently. (Polenta is ready when wooden spoon stands upright in center of mixture.)

4. Add bell pepper mixture and Parmesan cheese to saucepan; stir to combine.

5. Spray 13×9×2-inch baking pan with nonstick cooking spray. Spread polenta evenly into baking pan. Cover; let stand at room temperature 6 hours or until completely cooled and firm.

6. Preheat oven to 350°F. Cut polenta into 24 squares. Pour spaghetti sauce evenly over polenta.

7. Bake 20 to 25 minutes until sauce is bubbly around edges of pan. Remove from oven. Sprinkle with provolone cheese.

8. Bake 2 to 3 minutes just until provolone cheese is melted. Let stand 5 minutes. Loosen polenta at edges with metal spatula.

9. Carefully lift polenta pieces out of pan with wide spatula. Garnish as desired.

makes 6 to 8 servings

**Polenta Squares with Chunky
Tomato Sauce**

Classic Pesto with Linguine

  ¾ pound uncooked linguine
  2 tablespoons butter or margarine
  ¼ cup plus 1 tablespoon olive oil, divided
  2 tablespoons pine nuts
  1 cup tightly packed fresh basil leaves, rinsed, drained and stemmed
  2 cloves garlic
  ¼ teaspoon salt
  ¼ cup freshly grated Parmesan cheese
  1½ tablespoons freshly grated Romano cheese
     Fresh basil leaves for garnish

1. Prepare linguine according to package directions; drain. Toss with butter in large serving bowl; set aside and keep warm.

2. Heat 1 tablespoon oil in small saucepan or skillet over medium-low heat. Add pine nuts; cook and stir 30 to 45 seconds until light brown, shaking pan constantly. Remove with slotted spoon; drain on paper towels.

3. Place toasted pine nuts, basil leaves, garlic and salt in food processor or blender. With processor running, add remaining ¼ cup oil in slow steady stream until evenly blended and pine nuts are finely chopped.

4. Transfer basil mixture to small bowl. Stir in Parmesan and Romano cheeses.*

5. Combine hot, buttered linguine and pesto sauce in large serving bowl; toss until well coated. Garnish, if desired. Serve immediately.

makes 4 servings (about ¾ cup pesto sauce)

*Pesto sauce can be stored at this point in airtight container; pour thin layer of olive oil over pesto and cover. Refrigerate up to 1 week. Bring to room temperature. Proceed as directed in step 5.

Classic Pesto with Linguine

Penne with Fresh Herb Tomato Sauce

1 pound uncooked penne pasta
4 ripe large tomatoes, peeled and seeded*
½ cup tomato sauce
¼ cup FILIPPO BERIO® Olive Oil
1 to 2 tablespoons lemon juice
2 teaspoons minced fresh parsley *or* 1 teaspoon dried parsley
1 teaspoon minced fresh rosemary, oregano or thyme or 1 teaspoon dried
    Italian seasoning
Salt and freshly ground black pepper
Shavings of Parmesan cheese

For chunkier sauce, reserve 1 peeled, seeded tomato. Finely chop; stir into sauce.

Cook pasta according to package directions until al dente (tender but still firm). Drain; transfer to large bowl. Process tomatoes in blender container or food processor until smooth. Add tomato sauce. While machine is running, very slowly add olive oil. Add lemon juice, parsley and herbs. Process briefly at high speed. Spoon sauce over hot or room temperature pasta. Season to taste with salt and pepper. Top with cheese. *makes 4 servings*

Penne with Fresh Herb Tomato Sauce

Pizza Romano

       1 cup water
       2 tablespoons peanut oil
  1½ teaspoons salt
       3 cups bread flour
       1 tablespoon sugar
       2 teaspoons FLEISCHMANN'S® Bread Machine Yeast

TOPPING
       1 can (15 ounces) crushed tomatoes
  ½ cup freshly grated Romano cheese
       1 tablespoon peanut oil
       1 teaspoon dried marjoram leaves
  ⅛ teaspoon ground black pepper
       2 cups sliced fresh mushrooms

Add water, oil, salt, flour, sugar, and yeast to bread machine pan in the order suggested by manufacturer. Select dough/manual cycle. When mix cycle is complete (before baking starts), remove dough from machine to lightly oiled surface. If necessary, knead in enough flour to make dough easy to handle.

Divide dough in half. Shape each half into a ball; roll each ball into 12-inch circle. Place on two greased baking sheets; form standing rim by pinching edge of dough. Prick dough with fork; let rest 10 minutes. Meanwhile, combine all topping ingredients except mushrooms in medium bowl.

Partially bake crusts at 450°F for 8 minutes. Remove crusts from baking sheets; place on wire cooling racks. Spread topping mixture evenly over each pizza crust. Sprinkle with mushrooms. Bake on wire racks of oven at 450°F for 12 to 14 minutes or until done. Cool slightly; cut into slices and serve.   *makes 2 (12-inch) pizzas*

Baked Bow-Tie Pasta in Mushroom Cream Sauce

        1 teaspoon olive or vegetable oil
        1 package (10 ounces) sliced mushrooms
        1 large onion, thinly sliced
        ⅛ teaspoon ground black pepper
        1 jar (16 ounces) RAGÚ® Cheese Creations!® Light Parmesan Alfredo Sauce
        8 ounces bow tie pasta, cooked and drained
        1 tablespoon grated Parmesan cheese
        1 tablespoon plain dry bread crumbs (optional)

1. Preheat oven to 400°F. In 10-inch nonstick skillet, heat oil over medium heat and cook mushrooms, onion and pepper, stirring frequently, 10 minutes or until vegetables are golden. Stir in Ragú Cheese Creations! Sauce.

2. In 2-quart shallow baking dish, combine sauce mixture with hot pasta. Sprinkle with cheese combined with bread crumbs. Cover with aluminum foil and bake 20 minutes. Remove foil and bake an additional 5 minutes.   *makes 6 servings*

prep time: 10 minutes
cook time: 35 minutes

Spinach Stuffed Manicotti

1 package (10 ounces) frozen spinach
8 uncooked manicotti shells
1½ teaspoons olive oil
1 teaspoon dried rosemary
1 teaspoon dried sage leaves
1 teaspoon dried oregano leaves
1 teaspoon dried thyme leaves
1 teaspoon chopped garlic
1½ cups chopped fresh tomatoes
½ cup ricotta cheese
½ cup fresh whole wheat bread crumbs
2 egg whites, lightly beaten
Yellow pepper rings and sage sprig for garnish

1. Cook spinach according to package directions. Place in colander to drain. Let stand until cool enough to handle. Squeeze spinach with hands to remove excess moisture. Set aside.

2. Cook pasta according to package directions; drain. Rinse under cold running water until cool enough to handle; drain.

3. Preheat oven to 350°F. Heat oil in small saucepan over medium heat. Cook and stir rosemary, sage, oregano, thyme and garlic in hot oil about 1 minute. *Do not let herbs brown.* Add tomatoes; reduce heat to low. Simmer, uncovered, 10 minutes, stirring occasionally.

4. Combine spinach, cheese and crumbs in bowl. Fold in egg whites. Fill shells with spinach mixture using spoon.

5. Place one third of tomato mixture on bottom of 13×9-inch baking pan. Arrange manicotti in pan. Pour tomato mixture over top. Cover with foil.

6. Bake 30 minutes or until bubbly. Garnish, if desired.   *makes 4 servings*

Spinach Stuffed Manicotti

Risotto alla Milanese

¼ teaspoon saffron threads, crushed to a powder
3½ to 4 cups chicken broth
7 tablespoons butter or margarine, divided
1 large onion, chopped
1½ cups uncooked arborio or short-grain white rice
½ cup dry white wine
½ teaspoon salt
Dash pepper
¼ cup freshly grated Parmesan cheese

1. Place saffron in glass measuring cup. Bring broth to a boil in small saucepan; reduce heat to low. Stir ½ cup broth into saffron to dissolve; set aside. Keep remaining broth hot.

2. Melt 6 tablespoons butter in 2½-quart saucepan over medium heat. Cook and stir onion in butter 5 minutes or until soft. Stir in rice; cook and stir 2 minutes. Stir in wine, salt and pepper. Cook, uncovered, 3 to 5 minutes until wine has evaporated, stirring occasionally.

3. Measure ½ cup hot broth; stir into rice mixture. Reduce heat to medium-low, maintaining a simmer throughout steps 4 and 5. Cook and stir until broth has absorbed. Repeat, adding ½ cup broth 3 more times, cooking and stirring until broth has absorbed.

4. Add saffron-flavored broth to rice and cook until absorbed. Continue adding remaining broth, ½ cup at a time, cooking and stirring until rice is tender but firm and mixture has slightly creamy consistency. (Not all the broth may be necessary. Total cooking time of rice will be about 20 minutes.) Remove risotto from heat. Stir in remaining 1 tablespoon butter and cheese. Garnish, if desired. Serve immediately. *makes 6 to 8 servings*

Tip

Saffron, the world's most expensive spice, flavors and tints food. Turmeric may be substituted to achieve the yellow color, but there is no substitute for the flavor.

Risotto alla Milanese

Ravioli with Tomato Pesto

 4 ounces frozen cheese ravioli
 1¼ cups coarsely chopped plum tomatoes
 ¼ cup fresh basil leaves
 2 teaspoons pine nuts
 2 teaspoons olive oil
 ¼ teaspoon salt
 ⅛ teaspoon black pepper
 1 tablespoon grated Parmesan cheese

1. Cook ravioli according to package directions; drain.

2. Meanwhile, combine tomatoes, basil, pine nuts, oil, salt and pepper in food processor. Process using on/off pulsing action just until ingredients are chopped. Serve over ravioli. Top with cheese. *makes 2 servings*

Penne Puttanesca

 3 tablespoons olive or vegetable oil
 2 cloves garlic, finely chopped
 1 jar (26 to 28 ounces) RAGÚ® Old World Style® Pasta Sauce
 ¼ cup chopped pitted oil-cured olives
 1 tablespoon capers, rinsed
 ½ teaspoon dried oregano leaves, crushed
 ¼ teaspoon crushed red pepper flakes
 1 box (16 ounces) penne pasta, cooked, drained

In 12-inch skillet, heat oil over low heat and cook garlic 30 seconds. Stir in remaining ingredients except pasta. Simmer uncovered, stirring occasionally, 15 minutes. Serve sauce over hot pasta. Garnish, if desired, with chopped fresh parsley. *makes 8 servings*

Ravioli with Tomato Pesto

Tri-Color Pasta

    1 package (16 ounces) tri-color pasta*
    2 cups BIRDS EYE® frozen Green Peas
    2 plum tomatoes, chopped *or* 1 red bell pepper, chopped
    1 cup shredded mozzarella cheese
    ⅓ cup, or to taste, prepared pesto sauce

Or, substitute 1 bag (16 ounces) frozen tortellini.

• In large saucepan, cook pasta according to package directions. Add peas during last 5 minutes; drain in colander. Rinse under cold water to cool.

• In large bowl, combine pasta, peas, tomatoes and cheese. Stir in pesto.

makes 4 servings

prep time: 5 minutes
cook time: 10 minutes

Tortellini with Creamy Pesto

    2 cups loosely packed fresh basil leaves
    1 cup loosely packed parsley
    ⅓ cup WISH-BONE® Italian Dressing*
    ½ cup whipping or heavy cream
    ¼ cup grated Parmesan cheese
    ⅛ teaspoon ground black pepper
    2 packages (15 ounces) frozen tortellini, cooked and drained**

Also terrific with WISH-BONE® Robusto Italian or Just 2 Good Italian Dressing.

**Substitution: Use 1 package (16 ounces) fettuccine noodles, cooked and drained and increase grated Parmesan cheese to ½ cup.*

In food processor or blender, process basil with parsley until blended. While processing, through feed cap, gradually add Italian dressing, cream, cheese and pepper until blended. Toss basil mixture with hot tortellini. Serve, if desired, with additional cheese, salt and pepper to taste. Top, if desired, with toasted pine nuts.   *makes about 6 servings*

Tri-Color Pasta

Four Cheese Stuffed Shells

  12 uncooked jumbo pasta shells
   1 container (15 ounces) low-fat ricotta cheese
   1 cup (4 ounces) shredded provolone cheese
  ¼ cup (1 ounce) grated Parmesan cheese
   1 egg
  ¼ cup chopped fresh parsley
   1 teaspoon dried basil leaves
  ¼ teaspoon minced dried garlic
     Dash salt and black pepper
1½ cups chunky spaghetti sauce, divided
  ½ cup (2 ounces) shredded mozzarella cheese

1. Cook shells according to package directions, cooking only 10 to 12 minutes. Rinse, drain and set aside.

2. Combine ricotta cheese, provolone cheese, Parmesan cheese, egg, parsley, basil, garlic, salt and pepper in medium bowl. Stir until well mixed.

3. Spread ½ cup spaghetti sauce on bottom of 8-inch square baking pan. Fill shells with ricotta mixture; place in prepared dish. Spread remaining 1 cup spaghetti sauce over shells. Cover tightly with foil. Refrigerate overnight.

4. Preheat oven to 350°F. Bake, covered, 30 minutes. Uncover and continue baking 15 to 20 minutes longer or until sauce bubbles. Remove from oven and sprinkle with mozzarella cheese. Return to oven 1 to 2 minutes or until cheese is melted. Serve immediately.

makes 4 servings (12 shells)

make-ahead time: up to 1 day before serving
final prep and cook time: 30 minutes

Four Cheese Stuffed Shells

Rotelle with Fresh Tomato Basil Sauce

1 cup chopped onion
3 cloves garlic, minced
¼ teaspoon ground black pepper
¼ cup FLEISCHMANN'S® Original Margarine
4 large tomatoes, peeled, seeded and chopped
1 tablespoon dried basil leaves *or* ¼ cup fresh chopped basil
1 teaspoon sugar
8 ounces rotelle pasta, cooked and drained

1. Cook and stir onion, garlic and pepper in margarine in large skillet over medium-high heat until onion is tender, about 3 minutes.

2. Add tomatoes, basil and sugar; heat to a boil. Reduce heat; cover and simmer for 15 to 20 minutes.

3. Toss tomato mixture with hot cooked rotelle. Serve immediately.   *makes 6 servings*

preparation time: 25 minutes
cook time: 18 minutes
total time: 43 minutes

Spinach Lasagna

5 lasagna noodles
  Nonstick cooking spray
2 cups sliced fresh mushrooms
1 cup chopped onion
1 cup chopped green bell pepper
2 cloves garlic, minced
2 cans (8 ounces each) no-salt-added tomato sauce
1 teaspoon chopped fresh basil *or* ¼ teaspoon dried basil leaves
1 teaspoon chopped fresh oregano *or* ¼ teaspoon dried oregano leaves
¼ teaspoon ground red pepper
1½ cups 1% low fat cottage cheese or light ricotta cheese
¼ cup grated Romano or Parmesan cheese
2 egg whites, beaten
3 tablespoons fine dry bread crumbs
1 package (10 ounces) frozen chopped spinach, thawed and well drained
¾ cup (3 ounces) shredded part-skim mozzarella cheese
¼ cup chopped fresh parsley

Prepare noodles according to package directions; drain. Rinse under cold water; drain.

Coat large skillet with cooking spray. Add mushrooms, onion, bell pepper and garlic; cook and stir over medium heat until vegetables are tender. Stir in tomato sauce, basil, oregano and red pepper. Bring to a boil over medium-high heat. Reduce heat to medium-low. Simmer, uncovered, 10 minutes, stirring occasionally.

Preheat oven to 350°F. Combine cottage cheese, Romano cheese, egg whites and bread crumbs in medium bowl. Stir spinach into cottage cheese mixture. Cut noodles in half crosswise. Spread ½ cup sauce in ungreased 8- or 9-inch square baking dish. Top with half the noodles, half the spinach mixture and half the remaining sauce. Repeat layers.

Cover and bake 45 minutes or until heated through. Sprinkle with mozzarella cheese. Bake, uncovered, 2 to 3 minutes more or until cheese melts. Sprinkle with parsley. Let stand 10 minutes before serving.   *makes 4 servings*

Pasta with Spinach and Ricotta

8 ounces uncooked tri-colored rotini
Nonstick cooking spray
1 box (10 ounces) frozen chopped spinach, thawed and drained
2 teaspoons bottled minced garlic
1 cup fat-free or part-skim ricotta cheese
½ cup water
3 tablespoons grated Parmesan cheese, divided

1. Cook pasta according to package directions; drain.

2. While pasta is cooking, coat skillet with cooking spray; heat over medium-low heat. Add spinach and garlic; cook and stir 5 minutes. Stir in ricotta cheese, water and half of Parmesan cheese; season with salt and pepper to taste.

3. Add pasta to skillet; stir until well blended. Sprinkle with remaining Parmesan cheese.

makes 4 servings

Baked Pasta Primavera Casserole

1 jar (26 to 28 ounces) RAGÚ® Old World Style® Pasta Sauce
2 cups shredded mozzarella cheese (about 8 ounces)
½ cup grated Parmesan cheese
1 bag (16 ounces) frozen Italian-style vegetables, thawed
8 ounces ziti or penne pasta, cooked and drained

1. Preheat oven to 350°F. In large bowl, combine Ragú Pasta Sauce, 1 cup mozzarella cheese and Parmesan cheese. Stir in vegetables and hot pasta.

2. In 2½-quart casserole, spoon pasta mixture; sprinkle with remaining 1 cup mozzarella cheese. Bake uncovered 30 minutes or until heated through.

makes 6 servings

prep time: 10 minutes
cook time: 30 minutes

Pasta with Spinach and Ricotta

Roma Tomato Pizzas

  2 loaves (1 pound each) frozen bread dough, thawed
⅓ cup olive oil
  2 cups thinly sliced onions
  2 cloves garlic, minced
12 Roma (Italian plum) tomatoes, sliced ⅛-inch thick
  1 teaspoon dried basil leaves
  1 teaspoon dried oregano leaves
    Black pepper
½ cup grated Parmesan cheese
  1 can (2¼ ounces) sliced, pitted ripe olives, drained
    Green and yellow bell pepper strips

Preheat oven to 450°F. Roll out each loaf on lightly floured surface into 15-inch circle; press each into greased 15-inch pizza pan or stretch into 15×10-inch baking pan. Crimp edges to form rim; prick several times with fork. Bake crusts 10 minutes. Remove from oven; set aside.

Reduce oven temperature to 400°F. Heat oil in large skillet over medium-high heat. Add onions and garlic; cook and stir 6 to 8 minutes or until onions are tender. Divided onion mixture (including olive oil) between crusts. Arrange tomato slices evenly over onion mixture. Sprinkle each pizza with ½ teaspoon basil leaves, ½ teaspoon oregano leaves and black pepper to taste. Sprinkle each pizza with ¼ cup Parmesan cheese. Top with olives and desired amount of bell peppers. Bake 10 to 15 minutes or until toppings are heated through.

makes 2 (15-inch) pizzas

Roma Tomato Pizza

Caponata-Style Fettuccine

1 medium eggplant (about 1 pound), cut into ¼-inch slices
1¼ teaspoons salt, divided
⅓ cup olive oil, divided
1 small green bell pepper, cored and sliced
1 medium onion, coarsely chopped
2 cloves garlic, minced
3 medium tomatoes (about 1 pound), seeded and coarsely chopped
⅓ cup raisins
⅓ cup halved pitted green olives
¼ cup balsamic or red wine vinegar
2 tablespoons capers (optional)
¼ teaspoon ground cinnamon
¼ teaspoon black pepper
10 ounces fresh spinach fettuccine, cooked, drained and kept warm

1. Place eggplant slices in large colander over bowl; sprinkle with 1 teaspoon salt. Drain 1 hour.

2. Place oven rack at lowest position. Preheat oven to 450°F. Place eggplant slices in a single layer on baking sheet or jelly-roll pan; brush both sides lightly with some of oil. Bake 10 minutes or until lightly browned on bottoms. Turn slices over; bake 5 minutes more or until tops are lightly browned and slices are softened; set aside.

3. Heat remaining oil in large skillet over medium-high heat. Add bell pepper; cook and stir 5 minutes or until pepper turns bright green. Remove pepper; set aside.

4. Add onion and garlic to same skillet; cook and stir 5 minutes or until onion is soft. Add tomatoes, raisins, olives, vinegar, capers, cinnamon, black pepper and remaining ¼ teaspoon salt. Cook until most of the liquid has evaporated.

5. Cut roasted eggplant slices into quarters; add to tomato mixture. Add bell pepper; cook until heated through. Serve over fettuccine. Garnish, if desired. *makes 4 servings*

note: Caponata is a Sicilian eggplant dish that may be served cold as an appetizer or on lettuce as a salad. Here it is made into a vegetarian sauce for pasta.

Caponata-Style Fettuccine

Lasagna à la Zucchini

8 (2-inch-wide) uncooked lasagna noodles
3 medium zucchini, cut into thin slices
1 can (16 ounces) Italian-style sliced stewed tomatoes, drained
¼ pound fresh mushrooms, cut into thin slices
1 small onion, chopped
2 cloves garlic, minced
1 teaspoon dried Italian seasoning
¼ teaspoon salt
⅛ teaspoon black pepper
1 can (6 ounces) tomato paste
1 container (16 ounces) small curd cottage cheese
6 eggs, lightly beaten
¼ cup freshly grated Parmesan cheese
2 cups (8 ounces) shredded mozzarella cheese

1. Preheat oven to 350°F.

2. Cook lasagna noodles according to package directions until tender but still firm. Drain; set aside.

3. Combine zucchini, tomatoes, mushrooms, onion, garlic, Italian seasoning, salt and pepper in large skillet. Cook over medium-high heat 5 to 7 minutes or until zucchini is tender. Stir in tomato paste; remove from heat.

4. Combine cottage cheese, eggs and Parmesan cheese in medium bowl; stir until well blended.

5. Place 4 noodles on bottom of greased 13×9-inch baking dish. Pour ½ of egg mixture evenly over noodles. Cover egg mixture with ½ of tomato mixture; sprinkle with 1½ cups mozzarella. Repeat layers with remaining ingredients, ending with ½ cup mozzarella.

6. Bake covered 30 minutes. Uncover; bake 10 minutes or until heated through. Let stand 10 minutes before serving. *makes 8 to 10 servings*

Lasagna à la Zucchini

Rigatoni with Fresh Tomatoes

        1 cup rigatoni or mostaccioli
          Nonstick cooking spray
     1/4 cup sliced green onions
        2 cloves garlic, minced
        1 cup sliced zucchini
        1 teaspoon chopped fresh basil *or* 1/4 teaspoon dried basil leaves
        1 teaspoon chopped fresh marjoram *or* 1/4 teaspoon dried marjoram leaves
     1/8 teaspoon salt
     1/8 teaspoon black pepper
        1 cup coarsely chopped seeded plum tomatoes
     1/4 cup (1 ounce) crumbled feta cheese or shredded part-skim mozzarella cheese

Prepare rigatoni according to package directions; drain.

Coat wok or large skillet with cooking spray; heat over medium-high heat. Add onions and garlic. Cook and stir 1 minute. Add zucchini, basil, marjoram, salt and pepper. Cook and stir 2 to 3 minutes or until zucchini is tender. Stir in tomatoes and pasta; heat through.

Divide pasta mixture among four plates; sprinkle with cheese.   *makes 4 servings*

Tip

Feta, a brine-cured Greek cheese made from goat's milk, is also popular in Italy, France and the United States. It has a sharp, tangy and salty flavor.

Rigatoni with Fresh Tomatoes

Linguine Frittata

8 ounces linguine
3 tablespoons olive oil, divided
1 cup chopped carrots
¼ cup chopped onion
2 cloves garlic, minced
½ pound asparagus, cut into 1-inch pieces
1 large red bell pepper, diced
1 medium tomato, seeded and chopped
1 teaspoon dried basil leaves
1 teaspoon dried marjoram leaves
1 teaspoon dried oregano leaves
5 eggs, beaten
¼ cup grated Parmesan cheese
½ teaspoon salt
¼ teaspoon black pepper

1. Cook linguine according to package directions. Drain in colander. Place in large bowl.

2. Heat 1 tablespoon oil in large skillet over medium heat until hot. Add carrots, onion and garlic; cook and stir 5 minutes or until carrots are crisp-tender. Add asparagus, bell pepper, tomato, basil, marjoram and oregano; cook and stir 5 minutes or until asparagus is crisp-tender. Add vegetable mixture to linguine in bowl; toss.

3. Beat eggs in medium bowl with wire whisk until frothy. Stir in cheese, salt and black pepper; pour over linguine mixture and toss.

4. Heat remaining 2 tablespoons oil in 12-inch nonstick skillet over medium heat until hot. Add linguine mixture, spreading evenly. Reduce heat to low. Cook 5 minutes or until browned on bottom. Place large rimless plate over skillet; invert frittata onto plate. Slide frittata back into skillet. Cook 5 minutes more or until browned on bottom and eggs are set. Slide frittata onto serving plate. Cut into wedges. *makes 6 to 8 servings*

Linguine Frittata

Tuscany Cavatelli

        16 ounces uncooked cavatelli, penne or ziti pasta
        1½ cups diced plum tomatoes, seeded
        ⅔ cup chopped pimiento-stuffed green olives
        ¼ cup drained capers
        2 tablespoons olive oil
        2 tablespoons grated Parmesan cheese
        2 tablespoons balsamic vinegar or red wine vinegar
        ½ teaspoon black pepper
        2 cloves garlic, minced

1. Cook pasta according to package directions. Drain; set aside.

2. Combine tomatoes, olives, capers, oil, cheese, vinegar, pepper and garlic in medium bowl. Stir in pasta until thoroughly coated. Serve warm or at room temperature.

makes 5 (2-cup) servings

note: Capers are the small, pea-sized buds of flowers from the caper bush. Found mostly in Central America and the Mediterranean, capers add pungency to sauces, dips and relishes. Usually these green buds are pickled and can be found in the condiment section of the supermarket.

Classic Risotto

        1 can (14½ ounces) chicken broth
        2 cups water
        ¼ cup I CAN'T BELIEVE IT'S NOT BUTTER!® Spread
        1 small onion, chopped
        1 clove garlic, finely chopped
        1 cup uncooked arborio or long grain rice
        ¼ cup dry white wine or chicken broth
        ¼ cup grated Parmesan cheese
        1 tablespoon finely chopped fresh parsley (optional)

continued on page 267

In 2-quart saucepan, bring broth and water to a boil; set aside.

In another 2-quart saucepan, melt I Can't Believe It's Not Butter! Spread over medium-high heat and cook onion and garlic, stirring occasionally, 2 minutes or until onion is tender. Stir in uncooked rice and cook, stirring occasionally, 2 minutes or until rice is golden. Stir in wine and cook 1 minute or until liquid is absorbed. Reduce heat to low and add hot broth mixture, ½ cup at a time, stirring constantly, until liquid is absorbed and rice is slightly creamy and just tender. Stir in cheese and parsley.   *makes 4 servings*

Pasta Roll-Ups

    1 package (1.5 ounces) LAWRY'S® Original-Style Spaghetti Sauce Spices & Seasonings
    1 can (6 ounces) tomato paste
2¼ cups water
    2 tablespoons butter or vegetable oil
    2 cups cottage cheese or ricotta cheese
    1 cup (4 ounces) shredded mozzarella cheese
    ¼ cup grated Parmesan cheese
    2 eggs, lightly beaten
    ½ to 1 teaspoon LAWRY'S® Garlic Salt
    ½ teaspoon dried basil, crushed (optional)
    8 ounces lasagna noodles, cooked and drained

In medium saucepan, prepare Spaghetti Sauce Spices & Seasonings according to package directions using tomato paste, water and butter. In large bowl, combine remaining ingredients except noodles; mix well. Spread ¼ cup cheese mixture on entire length of each lasagna noodle; roll up. Place noodles, seam side down, in microwave-safe baking dish. Cover with vented plastic wrap and microwave on HIGH 6 to 7 minutes or until cheese begins to melt. Pour sauce over rolls and microwave on HIGH 1 minute longer, if necessary, to heat sauce.   *makes 6 servings*

serving suggestion: Sprinkle with additional grated Parmesan cheese. Garnish with fresh basil leaves.

Fettuccine Gorgonzola with Sun-Dried Tomatoes

8 ounces uncooked spinach or tri-color fettuccine
1 cup low-fat cottage cheese
½ cup plain nonfat yogurt
½ cup (2 ounces) crumbled Gorgonzola cheese
⅛ teaspoon white pepper
2 cups rehydrated sun-dried tomatoes (4 ounces dry), cut into strips

1. Cook pasta according to package directions. Drain well. Cover to keep warm.

2. Combine cottage cheese and yogurt in food processor or blender; process until smooth. Heat cottage cheese mixture in small saucepan over low heat. Add Gorgonzola and white pepper; stir until cheese is melted.

3. Return pasta to saucepan; add tomatoes. Pour cheese mixture over pasta; mix well. Garnish as desired. Serve immediately.   *makes 4 servings*

Penne Pasta with Portobello Mushroom Tomato Sauce

1 tablespoon margarine or butter
2 medium portobello mushrooms, stems removed and coarsely chopped
1 tablespoon balsamic vinegar
1 jar (26 to 28 ounces) RAGÚ® Light Pasta Sauce
¼ teaspoon ground black pepper
1 box (16 ounces) penne or ziti pasta, cooked and drained

In 12-inch skillet, melt margarine over medium heat and cook mushrooms, stirring occasionally, 7 minutes or until tender. Stir in vinegar and cook, stirring constantly, 1 minute. Stir in pasta sauce and pepper; simmer uncovered, stirring occasionally, 15 minutes. Serve over hot pasta and garnish, if desired, with fresh grated Parmesan cheese.

makes 8 servings

Fettuccine Gorgonzola with Sun-Dried Tomatoes

Pasta Primavera

8 ounces uncooked mafalda pasta
2 medium zucchini (about 1 pound)
3 tablespoons roasted garlic-flavored vegetable oil
1 red bell pepper, thinly sliced
½ cup loosely packed fresh basil leaves, coarsely chopped
½ cup grated Parmesan cheese

1. Cook pasta according to package directions; drain. Place in large bowl.

2. While pasta is cooking, cut zucchini lengthwise into halves. Cut crosswise into thin slices.

3. Heat oil in large skillet over medium-high heat until hot. Add zucchini and bell pepper; cook 3 to 4 minutes until vegetables are crisp-tender, stirring frequently.

4. Add zucchini mixture and basil to pasta; toss gently until well combined. Season to taste with salt and black pepper. Serve with cheese. *makes 4 servings*

Pesto Pasta

1 cup packed fresh basil leaves
1 cup KRAFT® 100% Grated Parmesan Cheese, divided
⅓ cup olive oil
¼ cup pine nuts
2 cloves garlic, minced
8 ounces radiatore pasta, cooked, drained
1 cup halved pitted ripe olives
1 cup chopped seeded tomatoes

PLACE basil, ¾ cup of cheese, oil, pine nuts and garlic in food processor container fitted with steel blade; cover. Process until smooth.

TOSS basil mixture with pasta, olives and tomato. Sprinkle with remaining ¼ cup cheese. *makes 4 servings*

prep time: 20 minutes

Pasta Primavera

Parmesan Polenta

4 cups chicken broth
1¼ cups yellow cornmeal
1 small onion, minced
4 cloves garlic, minced
1 tablespoon minced fresh rosemary *or* 1 teaspoon dried rosemary
½ teaspoon salt
6 tablespoons grated Parmesan cheese
1 tablespoon olive oil, divided

1. Spray 11×7-inch baking pan with nonstick cooking spray; set aside. Spray one side of 7-inch-long sheet of waxed paper with cooking spray; set aside. Combine chicken broth, cornmeal, onion, garlic, rosemary and salt in medium saucepan. Cover and bring to a boil over high heat. Reduce heat to medium and simmer 10 to 15 minutes or until mixture has consistency of thick mashed potatoes. Remove from heat and stir in cheese.

2. Spread polenta evenly in prepared pan; place waxed paper, sprayed-side down, on polenta and smooth. (If surface is bumpy, it is more likely to stick to grill.) Cool on wire rack 15 minutes or until firm. Remove waxed paper; cut into 6 squares. Remove squares from pan.

3. To prevent sticking, spray grid with cooking spray. Prepare coals for grilling. Brush tops of squares with half the oil. Grill oil-side down on covered grill over medium to low coals for 6 to 8 minutes or until golden. Brush with remaining oil and gently turn over. Grill 6 to 8 minutes more or until golden. Serve warm. *makes 6 servings*

Parmesan Polenta

Vegetable Risotto

2 cups broccoli florets
1 cup finely chopped zucchini
1 cup finely chopped yellow squash
1 cup finely chopped red bell pepper
2½ cups chicken broth
1 tablespoon extra virgin olive oil
2 tablespoons finely chopped onion
½ cup arborio or other short-grain rice
¼ cup dry white wine or water
⅓ cup freshly grated Parmesan cheese

1. Steam broccoli, zucchini, yellow squash and bell pepper 3 minutes or just until crisp-tender. Rinse with cold water; drain and set aside.

2. Bring broth to a simmer in small saucepan; keep hot on low heat. Heat oil in heavy large saucepan over medium-high heat until hot. Add onion; reduce heat to medium. Cook and stir about 5 minutes or until onion is translucent. Add rice, stirring to coat with oil. Add wine; cook and stir until almost dry. Add ½ cup hot broth; cook and stir until broth is absorbed. Continue adding broth, ½ cup at a time, allowing broth to absorb before each addition and stirring frequently. (Total cooking time for broth absorption is about 20 minutes.)

3. Remove from heat and stir in cheese. Add steamed vegetables and mix well. Serve immediately.

makes 6 servings

Tip

Arborio is a short-grain Italian rice that is high in starch. It is traditionally used to make risotto, because it produces the characteristic creamy texture. If it is not available, substitute a short-grain rice rather than a long-grain one.

Vegetable Risotto

Sun-Dried Tomato Pesto with Tortellini

2 packages (9 ounces each) refrigerated three-cheese tortellini
¼ cup slivered almonds or walnuts
10 oil-packed sun-dried tomatoes
½ cup fresh parsley leaves, coarsely chopped
¼ cup fresh basil leaves, coarsely chopped
¼ cup grated Parmesan cheese
3 cloves garlic
2 teaspoons olive oil

1. Cook pasta according to package directions.

2. Meanwhile, toast almonds in heavy skillet over low heat 3 to 4 minutes or until lightly browned, stirring frequently. Remove almonds from skillet; cool.

3. Combine tomatoes, almonds, parsley, basil, Parmesan cheese, garlic and oil in food processor or blender; process until well blended. (If pesto is too dry, add hot pasta cooking water, 1 teaspoon at a time, until desired consistency.)

4. Combine tortellini and pesto in serving bowl; toss to combine. Garnish with fresh basil, if desired.   *makes 6 servings*

For a special touch, top tortellini with fresh basil leaves.

prep and cook time: 20 minutes

Sun-Dried Tomato Pesto with Tortellini

Vegetable Calzones

1 loaf (1 pound) frozen bread dough
1 package (10 ounces) frozen chopped broccoli, thawed and well drained
1 cup (8 ounces) ricotta cheese
1 cup (4 ounces) shredded BELGIOIOSO® Sharp Provolone Cheese
1 clove garlic, minced
¼ teaspoon black pepper
1 egg
1 tablespoon water
1 jar spaghetti sauce
    Grated BELGIOIOSO® Parmesan Cheese

Thaw bread dough; let rise according to package directions. Combine broccoli, ricotta, BelGioioso Provolone Cheese, garlic and pepper. Punch down bread dough; turn out onto lightly floured surface. Divide into 4 equal pieces. Roll out each piece into 8-inch circle. Place about ¼ cup cheese mixture on half of circle, leaving 1-inch border. Fold dough over to cover filling, forming semicircle; press edges with fork tines to seal.

Beat egg and water in small bowl. Brush with egg mixture. Place on greased baking sheet. Bake at 350°F 30 minutes or until brown and puffed. Transfer to rack; cool 10 minutes. Heat spaghetti sauce until hot and pour over calzones. Top with BelGioioso Parmesan Cheese.

makes 4 servings

Linguine with Asparagus and Asiago

1 pound fresh asparagus, cut into 1-inch pieces
16 ounces uncooked linguine, broken in half
1 tablespoon butter or margarine
1 cup (4 ounces) shredded Asiago or grated Parmesan cheese
½ cup sour cream
½ cup pitted black olive slices

Place 3 quarts of water in Dutch oven; cover and bring to a boil over high heat. Drop asparagus into boiling water; boil 1 to 2 minutes or until crisp-tender. Remove with slotted spoon; rinse under cold water. Drain.

continued on page 279

Add linguine to boiling water; cook according to package directions until al dente. Drain.

Combine linguine and butter in large bowl; toss gently until butter is melted. Add asparagus, cheese, sour cream and olives; toss gently until linguine is coated and cheese is melted. Season to taste with salt and pepper. Serve immediately.   *makes 4 servings*

prep and cook time: 30 minutes

Meatless Ravioli Bake

4 cups finely chopped eggplant
½ cup chopped onion
¼ cup chopped carrots
¼ cup chopped celery
3 tablespoons olive oil
2 (8-ounce) cans HUNT'S® No Salt Added Tomato Sauce
1 (14.5-ounce) can HUNT'S® Crushed Tomatoes
½ teaspoon sugar
⅛ teaspoon pepper
1 (18-ounce) package frozen large ravioli, prepared according to package directions

1. Preheat oven to 375°F.

2. In saucepan, sauté eggplant, onion, carrots and celery in hot oil; cook until tender.

3. Stir in Hunt's Tomato Sauce, Hunt's Tomatoes, sugar and pepper. Simmer, uncovered, 10 minutes; stirring occasionally.

4. Spoon *1½ cups* of tomato mixture into 13×9×2-inch baking dish; top with half the ravioli and *half* of the *remaining* sauce. Repeat layers.

5. Bake, uncovered, 30 minutes or until bubbly.   *makes 6 (7-ounce) servings*

Triple-Pepper Fettuccine

1 medium green bell pepper, cut into strips
1 medium red bell pepper, cut into strips
1 medium yellow bell pepper, cut into strips
2 cloves garlic, minced
¼ cup margarine
1 cup chicken broth
½ cup GREY POUPON® Dijon Mustard
1 (12-ounce) package fettuccine, cooked and drained

1. Cook and stir peppers and garlic in margarine in skillet over medium heat until tender-crisp, about 2 minutes; remove from skillet.

2. Blend chicken broth and mustard in same skillet. Heat to a boil; reduce heat. Simmer, stirring occasionally, for 3 to 4 minutes or until slightly thickened.

3. Return peppers to skillet; heat through. Toss with hot fettuccine and serve immediately.

makes 4 servings

preparation time: 15 minutes
cook time: 15 minutes
total time: 30 minutes

Triple-Pepper Fettuccine

Quattro Formaggio Pizza

1 (12-inch) Italian bread shell
½ cup prepared pizza or marinara sauce
4 ounces shaved or thinly sliced provolone cheese
1 cup (4 ounces) shredded smoked or regular mozzarella cheese
2 ounces Asiago or brick cheese, thinly sliced
¼ cup freshly grated Parmesan or Romano cheese

1. Heat oven to 450°F.

2. Place bread shell on baking sheet. Spread pizza sauce evenly over bread shell.

3. Top sauce with provolone, mozzarella, Asiago and Parmesan cheese.

4. Bake 14 minutes or until bread shell is golden brown and cheese is melted.

5. Cut into wedges; serve immediately.   *makes 4 servings*

serving suggestion: Serve with a tossed green salad.

prep and cook time: 26 minutes

Quattro Formaggio Pizza

Healthy Fettuccine Primavera

1 can (10¾ ounces) reduced-fat condensed cream of chicken soup
⅓ cup fat-free (skim) milk
2 cloves garlic, minced
½ teaspoon salt
½ teaspoon dried Italian seasoning
⅛ teaspoon fennel seeds, crushed
    Nonstick cooking spray
4 cups sliced fresh vegetables (peppers, zucchini, carrots, asparagus) or thawed
    frozen vegetables
1 cup coarsely chopped fresh plum tomatoes
4 cups hot cooked fettuccine

Combine soup, milk, garlic, salt, Italian seasoning and fennel seeds in small bowl; set aside.
Spray large nonstick skillet with cooking spray. Sauté vegetables over medium heat 4 to
5 minutes.* Stir in soup mixture; simmer 3 to 4 minutes. Add tomato; mix well. Serve over
hot fettuccine.   *makes 6 servings*

*You may add ½ pound cooked chicken, turkey sausage or shrimp at this point.

Healthy Fettuccine Primavera

SIDE DISHES

Lemon and Fennel Marinated Vegetables

1 cup water
2 medium carrots, diagonally sliced ½ inch thick
1 cup small whole fresh mushrooms
1 small red or green bell pepper, cut into ¾-inch pieces
3 tablespoons lemon juice
1 tablespoon sugar
1 tablespoon olive oil
1 clove garlic, minced
½ teaspoon fennel seeds, crushed
½ teaspoon dried basil leaves
¼ teaspoon black pepper

Bring water to a boil over high heat in small saucepan. Add carrots. Return to a boil. Reduce heat to medium-low. Cover and simmer about 5 minutes or until carrots are crisp-tender. Drain and cool.

Place carrots, mushrooms and bell pepper in large resealable plastic food storage bag. Combine lemon juice, sugar, oil, garlic, fennel seeds, basil and black pepper in small bowl. Pour over vegetables. Close bag securely; turn to coat. Marinate in refrigerator 8 to 24 hours, turning occasionally.

Drain vegetables; discard marinade. Place vegetables in serving dish.   *makes 4 servings*

Lemon and Fennel Marinated
Vegetables

Baked Tomato Risotto

1 jar (28 ounces) spaghetti sauce
1 can (14 ounces) chicken broth
2 cups halved sliced zucchini
1 can (4 ounces) sliced mushrooms
1 cup arborio rice
2 cups (8 ounces) shredded mozzarella cheese

Preheat oven to 350°F. Spray 3-quart casserole with nonstick cooking spray.

Combine spaghetti sauce, broth, zucchini, mushrooms and rice in prepared dish.

Bake, covered, 30 minutes. Remove from oven and stir casserole. Cover and bake 15 to 20 minutes more or until rice is tender. Remove from oven; sprinkle evenly with cheese. Bake, uncovered, 5 minutes or until cheese is melted. *makes 6 servings*

Herbed Green Beans

1 pound fresh green beans, stem ends removed
1 teaspoon extra virgin olive oil
2 tablespoons chopped fresh basil *or* 2 teaspoons dried basil leaves

1. Steam green beans 5 minutes or until crisp-tender. Rinse under cold running water; drain and set aside.

2. Just before serving, heat oil over medium-low heat in large nonstick skillet. Add basil; cook and stir 1 minute, then add green beans. Cook until heated through. Garnish with additional fresh basil, if desired. Serve immediately. *makes 6 servings*

cook's tip: When buying green beans, look for vivid green, crisp beans without scars. Pods should be well shaped and slim with small seeds. Buy beans of uniform size to ensure even cooking and avoid bruised or large beans.

Baked Tomato Risotto

Pepper-Stuffed Artichokes

4 large artichokes, outer leaves removed
¼ cup lemon juice
2 teaspoons olive oil
½ cup chopped onion
2 cloves garlic, minced
½ cup diced red bell pepper
½ cup diced yellow bell pepper
½ cup fresh whole wheat bread crumbs
2 tablespoons chopped fresh parsley
2 teaspoons dried oregano leaves
⅛ teaspoon black pepper
1 can (14½ ounces) no-salt-added peeled tomatoes, undrained
2 tablespoons freshly grated Parmesan cheese

1. Preheat oven to 350°F. Trim 1 inch off top and stem of each artichoke. Dip artichokes in lemon juice to prevent browning.

2. Bring 5 cups water to boil in large saucepan over high heat. Reduce heat to low; add artichokes and simmer 30 minutes. Drain and cool slightly. Cut in half lengthwise. Scoop out and discard center of artichoke.

3. Heat oil in small nonstick skillet over medium heat. Add onion and garlic; cook and stir 3 to 4 minutes or until onion is tender. Remove from heat; stir in bell peppers, bread crumbs, parsley, oregano and black pepper. Stuff artichokes with bell pepper mixture.

4. Spray 9-inch square baking pan with nonstick cooking spray. Arrange stuffed artichokes in prepared pan. Set aside.

5. Place tomatoes with juice in food processor or blender; process until smooth. Pour over artichokes. Sprinkle with Parmesan. Cover and bake 30 minutes or until lightly browned.

makes 4 servings

Pepper-Stuffed Artichoke

Italian Green Beans

½ cup water
1 package (16 ounces) frozen whole green beans
½ cup cubed POLLY-O® Non-Fat Mozzarella Cheese (¼-inch cubes)
½ cup chopped seeded tomato
⅓ cup KRAFT FREE® Italian Fat Free Dressing

BRING water to boil in medium saucepan. Add green beans; cook 2 minutes or until tender. Drain.

STIR in cheese, tomato and dressing. Serve hot.   *makes 6 servings*

prep: 5 minutes
cook: 10 minutes

Marinated Tomatoes & Mozzarella

1 cup chopped fresh basil leaves
1 pound Italian tomatoes, sliced
½ pound fresh packed buffalo mozzarella cheese, sliced
¼ cup olive oil
3 tablespoons chopped fresh chives
2 tablespoons red wine vinegar
2 teaspoons sugar
½ teaspoon dried oregano
½ teaspoon LAWRY'S® Seasoned Pepper
½ teaspoon LAWRY'S® Garlic Powder with Parsley
Fresh basil leaves (optional)

In large resealable plastic food storage bag, combine all ingredients except whole basil leaves; mix well. Marinate in refrigerator at least 30 minutes. To serve, arrange tomato and cheese slices on serving plate. Garnish with whole basil leaves, if desired.   *makes 4 to 6 servings*

serving suggestion: Serve with grilled chicken sandwiches or as a zesty Italian appetizer.

Italian Green Beans

Fried Eggplant

1 medium eggplant (about 1 pound)
1 teaspoon salt
6 ounces mozzarella cheese
½ teaspoon active dry yeast
1½ cups warm water (105°F to 115°F)
2 cups all-purpose flour, divided
⅛ teaspoon black pepper
4½ tablespoons olive oil, divided
2 tablespoons minced fresh basil *or* ½ teaspoon dried basil leaves
Vegetable oil
1 egg white
Lemon slices (optional)

1. Rinse eggplant; cut crosswise into ¼-inch-thick slices. Place in large colander over bowl; sprinkle with salt. Drain 1 hour.

2. Cut cheese into ⅛-inch-thick slices. Trim cheese slices to size of eggplant slices. Wrap in plastic; set aside.

3. Sprinkle yeast over warm water in medium bowl; stir until dissolved. Whisk in 1½ cups flour and pepper until smooth. Let batter stand at room temperature 30 minutes.

4. Rinse eggplant and drain well; pat slices dry between paper towels. Heat 1½ tablespoons olive oil in large skillet over medium-high heat; add as many eggplant slices in single layer without crowding. Cook 2 minutes per side until slices are light brown. Remove with slotted spatula; drain on paper towels. Repeat with remaining olive oil and eggplant slices.

5. Sprinkle cheese slices with basil. Place each cheese slice between 2 eggplant slices; press firmly together. Spread remaining ½ cup flour on plate. Dip eggplant stacks in flour to coat lightly.

6. Heat 1½ inches vegetable oil in large saucepan to 350°F. Adjust heat to maintain temperature. Beat egg white in small bowl with electric mixer at high speed until stiff peaks form; fold into yeast batter. Dip eggplant stacks, 1 at a time, into batter; gently shake off excess. Fry stacks in oil, 3 at a time, 2 minutes per side until browned. Remove with slotted spatula; drain on paper towels. Serve hot with lemon slices. Garnish, if desired.

makes 4 to 6 servings

Fried Eggplant

Zucchini Tomato Bake

1 pound eggplant, coarsely chopped
2 cups zucchini slices
2 cups mushrooms slices
2 teaspoons olive oil
½ cup chopped onion
½ cup chopped fresh fennel (optional)
2 cloves garlic, minced
1 can (14½ ounces) no-salt-added whole tomatoes, undrained
1 tablespoon no-salt-added tomato paste
2 teaspoons dried basil leaves
1 teaspoon sugar

1. Preheat oven to 350°F. Arrange eggplant, zucchini and mushrooms in 9-inch square baking dish.

2. Heat oil in small skillet over medium heat. Add onion, fennel, if desired, and garlic. Cook and stir 3 to 4 minutes or until onion is tender. Add tomatoes with juice, tomato paste, basil and sugar. Cook and stir about 4 minutes or until sauce thickens.

3. Pour sauce over eggplant mixture. Cover and bake 30 minutes. Cool slightly before serving. Garnish as desired. *makes 6 servings*

Tip

The common western eggplant is available all year with the peak months being August and September. Italian eggplant looks like a miniature version of the western eggplant; it has a more delicate skin and flesh. They are less readily available than western eggplants. Look for them in large supermarkets, specialty produce markets or farmers' markets.

Zucchini Tomato Bake

Artichoke Hearts Marinara

1 pound baby artichokes (about 12)
1 lemon half
2 tablespoons olive oil
½ cup chopped onion
1 clove garlic, minced
½ cup chicken broth
1 cup prepared marinara or spaghetti sauce
¼ cup freshly grated Parmesan cheese
Lemon wedges and artichoke leaves for garnish

1. To prepare baby artichokes, rinse under running water. Bend back outer leaves and snap off at base. Continue snapping off leaves until top halves of leaves are green and bottom halves are yellow.

2. Cut off green fibrous tips of leaves, parallel to base. Cut stem off, level with base. Cut in half from top to bottom. To prevent discoloration, rub ends with lemon.

3. Heat oil in large skillet over medium-high heat. Cook and stir artichoke hearts, onion and garlic 5 to 10 minutes until onion is golden. Add broth; cover. Bring to a boil over high heat; reduce heat and simmer 10 to 15 minutes. Uncover; simmer until liquid has evaporated.

4. Preheat broiler. Spread marinara sauce in 8-inch-square broilerproof baking dish or 4 individual broilerproof serving dishes. Arrange artichoke hearts cut side down in sauce. Sprinkle with cheese. Brown under broiler about 5 minutes or until sauce is heated through and cheese is melted. Garnish, if desired. Serve immediately.   *makes 4 servings*

Italian Broccoli with Tomatoes

   4 cups broccoli florets
½ cup water
½ teaspoon dried Italian seasoning
½ teaspoon dried parsley flakes
¼ teaspoon salt (optional)
⅛ teaspoon black pepper
   2 medium tomatoes, cut into wedges
½ cup shredded part-skim mozzarella cheese

MICROWAVE DIRECTIONS
Place broccoli and water in 2-quart microwavable casserole; cover. Microwave at HIGH (100% power) 5 to 8 minutes or until crisp-tender. Drain. Stir in Italian seasoning, parsley, salt, pepper and tomatoes. Microwave, uncovered, at HIGH (100% power) 2 to 4 minutes or until tomatoes are hot. Sprinkle with cheese. Microwave 1 minute or until cheese melts.

makes 6 servings

Parmesano Zucchini

   2 tablespoons olive oil
   2 medium zucchini, cut into julienne strips
   1 small red onion, thinly sliced
   6 ounces sliced fresh mushrooms (about 2 cups)
¼ cup chopped fresh basil leaves
½ teaspoon LAWRY'S® Garlic Powder with Parsley
½ teaspoon LAWRY'S® Seasoned Salt
⅓ cup freshly grated Parmesan cheese

In medium skillet, heat oil; add all remaining ingredients except cheese. Cook 3 minutes or until zucchini is tender. Sprinkle with Parmesan cheese just before serving.

makes 4 servings

Oven-Roasted Peppers and Onions

Olive oil cooking spray
2 medium green bell peppers
2 medium red bell peppers
2 medium yellow bell peppers
4 small onions
1 teaspoon Italian herb seasoning
½ teaspoon dried basil leaves
¼ teaspoon ground cumin

1. Preheat oven to 375°F. Spray 15×10-inch jelly-roll pan with cooking spray. Cut bell peppers into 1½-inch pieces. Cut onions into quarters. Place vegetables on prepared pan. Spray vegetables with cooking spray. Bake 20 minutes; stir. Sprinkle with herb blend, basil and cumin.

2. *Increase oven temperature to 425°F.* Bake 20 minutes or until edges are darkened and vegetables are crisp-tender.   *makes 6 servings*

Green Beans with Pine Nuts

1 pound green beans, ends removed
2 tablespoons butter or margarine
2 tablespoons pine nuts
Salt
Pepper

Cook beans in 1 inch water in covered 3-quart pan 4 to 8 minutes or until crisp-tender; drain. Melt butter in large skillet over medium heat. Add pine nuts; cook, stirring frequently, until golden. Add beans; stir gently to coat beans with butter. Season with salt and pepper to taste.
                                                            makes 4 servings

Oven-Roasted Peppers and Onions

Broccoli Casserole with Crumb Topping

2 slices day-old white bread, coarsely crumbled (about 1¼ cups)
½ cup shredded mozzarella cheese (about 2 ounces)
2 tablespoons chopped fresh parsley (optional)
2 tablespoons olive or vegetable oil
1 clove garlic, finely chopped
6 cups broccoli florets and/or cauliflowerets
1 envelope LIPTON® RECIPE SECRETS® Onion Soup Mix*
1 cup water
1 large tomato, chopped

*Also terrific with LIPTON® RECIPE SECRETS® Garlic Mushroom Soup Mix.

1. In small bowl, combine bread crumbs, cheese, parsley, 1 tablespoon oil and garlic; set aside.

2. In 12-inch skillet, heat remaining 1 tablespoon oil over medium heat and cook broccoli, stirring frequently, 2 minutes.

3. Stir in soup mix blended with water. Bring to a boil over high heat. Reduce heat to low and simmer uncovered, stirring occasionally, 8 minutes or until broccoli is almost tender. Add tomato and simmer 2 minutes.

4. Spoon vegetable mixture into 1½-quart casserole; top with bread crumb mixture. Broil 1½ minutes or until crumbs are golden and cheese is melted. *makes 6 servings*

Broccoli Casserole with Crumb Topping

Vegetables with Spinach Fettuccine

6 solid-pack sun-dried tomatoes
3 ounces uncooked spinach florentine fettuccine or spinach fettuccine
1 tablespoon olive oil
¼ cup chopped onion
¼ cup sliced red bell pepper
1 clove garlic, minced
½ cup sliced mushrooms
½ cup coarsely chopped fresh spinach
¼ teaspoon salt
¼ teaspoon ground nutmeg
⅛ teaspoon black pepper

1. Place sun-dried tomatoes in small bowl; pour boiling water over tomatoes to cover. Let stand 10 to 15 minutes or until tomatoes are tender. Drain tomatoes; discard liquid. Cut tomatoes into strips.

2. Cook pasta according to package directions. Drain.

3. Heat oil in large nonstick skillet over medium heat until hot. Add onion, bell pepper and garlic; cook and stir 3 minutes or until vegetables are crisp-tender. Add mushrooms and spinach; cook and stir 1 minute. Add sun-dried tomatoes, pasta, salt, nutmeg and black pepper; cook and stir 1 to 2 minutes or until heated through. Garnish as desired.

makes 6 servings

Vegetables with Spinach Fettuccine

Broccoli and Cauliflower Linguine

2 tablespoons olive or vegetable oil
2 cups broccoli flowerets
2 cups cauliflowerets
3 cloves garlic, minced
2 cans (14.5 ounces each) CONTADINA® Recipe Ready Diced Tomatoes with
    Italian Herbs, undrained
1 teaspoon salt
¼ teaspoon crushed red pepper flakes
½ cup dry sherry or chicken broth
1 pound dry linguine, cooked, drained, kept warm
½ cup (2 ounces) grated Romano cheese
½ cup finely chopped fresh cilantro

1. Heat oil in large skillet. Add broccoli, cauliflower and garlic; sauté 3 minutes. Add tomatoes and juice, salt and red pepper flakes.

2. Bring to boil. Reduce heat; simmer, uncovered, 20 minutes, stirring occasionally.

3. Add sherry; simmer 3 minutes. In large bowl, place pasta. Add vegetable mixture, cheese and cilantro; toss to coat well. *makes 8 servings*

Orzo Casserole

2 tablespoons margarine or butter
1 clove garlic, finely chopped
1½ cups uncooked orzo pasta
1 envelope LIPTON® RECIPE SECRETS® Onion or Onion-Mushroom Soup Mix
3¼ cups water
6 ounces shiitake or white mushrooms, sliced
¼ cup chopped fresh parsley

continued on page 307

Orzo Casserole, continued

In 3-quart heavy saucepan, melt margarine over medium heat and cook garlic with orzo, stirring constantly, 2½ minutes or until golden. Stir in soup mix blended with water. Bring to a boil over high heat. Reduce heat to low and simmer, covered, 10 minutes. Add mushrooms; *do not stir.* Simmer, covered, 10 minutes. Stir in parsley. Turn into serving bowl. (Liquid will not be totally absorbed.) Let stand 10 minutes or until liquid is absorbed.

makes about 10 (½-cup) servings

savory orzo casserole: Increase water to 4 cups and use LIPTON® Recipe Secrets® Savory Herb with Garlic Soup Mix.

Orzo with Spinach and Red Pepper

    4 ounces uncooked orzo
      Nonstick cooking spray
    1 teaspoon olive oil
    1 medium red bell pepper, diced
    3 cloves garlic, minced
    1 package (10 ounces) frozen chopped spinach, thawed and squeezed dry
    ¼ cup grated Parmesan cheese
    ½ teaspoon minced fresh oregano or basil (optional)
    ¼ teaspoon lemon pepper

1. Prepare orzo according to package directions; drain well and set aside.

2. Spray large nonstick skillet with cooking spray. Heat skillet over medium-high heat until hot and add oil, tilting skillet to coat bottom. Add bell pepper and garlic; cook and stir 2 to 3 minutes or until bell pepper is crisp-tender. Add orzo and spinach; stir until evenly mixed and heated through. Remove from heat and stir in Parmesan cheese, oregano, if desired, and lemon pepper. Garnish as desired.

makes 6 servings

Pasta with Zesty Tomato Pesto

1 jar (8 ounces) sun-dried tomatoes, in oil, undrained
⅓ cup *French's®* Hearty Deli Brown Mustard
¼ cup grated Parmesan cheese
2 tablespoons pine nuts or slivered almonds
1 tablespoon *Frank's® RedHot®* Sauce
1 clove garlic, coarsely chopped
1 box (16 ounces) uncooked bow-tie pasta

1. Combine sun-dried tomatoes with oil, 1 cup water, mustard, Parmesan, pine nuts, *RedHot* Sauce and garlic in blender or food processor. Cover; process until well blended.

2. Cook pasta according to package directions; drain well. Place in large bowl. Pour sauce over pasta; toss well to coat evenly. Serve warm or at room temperature.

makes 6 side-dish servings (2 cups pesto)

note: If you enjoy the taste of pesto sauce, try adding ¼ cup *French's®* Dijon Mustard to 1 cup prepared pesto to make a spicy pesto dip or spread.

prep time: 15 minutes
cook time: 10 minutes

Pasta with Zesty Tomato Pesto

Risotto-Style Primavera

    1 tablespoon FILIPPO BERIO® Olive Oil
    1 small zucchini, sliced
    1 medium onion, sliced
    ½ red bell pepper, seeded and cut into thin strips
    3 mushrooms, sliced
    ½ cup uncooked long grain rice
    ¼ cup dry white wine
    1 cup chicken broth
  1¾ cups water, divided
    2 tablespoons grated Parmesan cheese
      Salt and freshly ground black pepper

In large saucepan or skillet, heat olive oil over medium heat until hot. Add zucchini, onion, bell pepper and mushrooms. Cook and stir 5 to 7 minutes or until zucchini is tender-crisp. Remove vegetables; set aside. Add rice and wine; stir until wine is absorbed. Add chicken broth. Cook, uncovered, stirring frequently, until absorbed. Add 1 cup water. Cook, uncovered, stirring frequently, until absorbed. Add remaining ¾ cup water. Cook, uncovered, stirring frequently, until absorbed. (Total cook time will be about 25 minutes until rice is tender and mixture is creamy.) Stir in vegetables and Parmesan cheese. Season to taste with salt and black pepper.

makes 4 servings

Risotto-Style Primavera

Antipasto Rice

1 cup MAHATMA® or CAROLINA® rice
1 (14½-ounce) can chicken broth
1 (14-ounce) can artichoke hearts, drained and quartered
1 (7-ounce) jar roasted bell peppers, drained and chopped
½ cup vegetable juice
1 teaspoon crushed basil leaves
1 teaspoon crushed oregano leaves
½ teaspoon salt (optional)
2 tablespoons snipped parsley
½ teaspoon pepper
¼ cup grated Parmesan cheese

In a large skillet, over medium heat, combine all ingredients, except Parmesan cheese. Bring to a boil. Reduce heat to simmer; cover. Simmer 20 minutes. Remove from heat. Fold in Parmesan cheese.   *makes 6 servings*

Tip

Roasted red peppers, which are sweet not hot, are available in jars in the canned vegetable or Italian food section of the supermarket. Roasting gives peppers a unique flavor. If you would like to roast peppers at home, see tip on page 318.

Rice Napoli

2 bags SUCCESS® Brown Rice
1 tablespoon reduced-calorie margarine
1 large green bell pepper, chopped
1 garlic clove, minced
1 can (14½ ounces) Italian-style tomatoes, drained
1 envelope (.7 ounce) Italian dressing mix
1 cup (4 ounces) shredded Mozzarella cheese
½ cup sliced pitted ripe olives (optional)

Prepare rice according to package directions.

Melt margarine in large skillet over medium-high heat. Add green pepper and garlic; cook and stir until pepper is crisp-tender. Add tomatoes and dressing. Bring to a boil. Reduce heat to low; simmer 10 minutes, stirring occasionally. Stir in rice. Top with cheese. Sprinkle with olives, if desired.

makes 8 servings

Spinach and Mushroom Risotto

        Nonstick olive oil cooking spray
½ pound mushrooms, sliced
2 teaspoons dried basil leaves
2 teaspoons minced garlic
¼ teaspoon black pepper
1 can (about 14 ounces) fat-free reduced-sodium chicken broth
1½ cups uncooked arborio rice
1 can (10¾ ounces) reduced-fat reduced-sodium condensed cream of
    mushroom soup, undiluted
1⅔ cups water
3 cups packed spinach leaves, chopped
6 tablespoons chopped walnuts, toasted
¼ cup grated Parmesan cheese

1. Spray 3-quart saucepan with cooking spray; heat over high heat. Add mushrooms, basil, garlic and pepper; cook and stir 3 to 4 minutes or until mushrooms are tender.

2. Stir in broth, rice, soup and water; cook and stir until well blended and mixture begins to boil. Reduce heat to low. Cover; simmer gently 12 minutes, stirring twice during cooking or until rice is just tender but still firm to the bite.

3. Stir in spinach; cover and let stand 5 to 7 minutes or until spinach is wilted.

4. Sprinkle with walnuts and cheese before serving.   *makes 8 (1-cup) servings*

Spinach and Mushroom Risotto

Mushroom Ragoût with Polenta

1 package (about ½ ounce) dried porcini mushrooms
½ cup boiling water
1 can (about 14 ounces) vegetable broth
½ cup yellow cornmeal
1 tablespoon olive oil
⅓ cup sliced shallots or chopped sweet onion
1 package (4 ounces) sliced mixed fresh exotic mushrooms or sliced cremini
    mushrooms
4 cloves garlic, minced
1 can (14½ ounces) Italian-style diced tomatoes, undrained
¼ teaspoon red pepper flakes
¼ cup chopped fresh basil or parsley
½ cup grated fat-free Parmesan cheese

1. Soak porcini mushrooms in boiling water 10 minutes.

2. Meanwhile, whisk together vegetable broth and cornmeal in large microwavable bowl. Cover with waxed paper; microwave at HIGH 5 minutes. Whisk well; cook at HIGH 3 to 4 minutes or until polenta is very thick. Whisk again; cover. Set aside.

3. Heat oil in large nonstick skillet over medium-high heat. Add shallots; cook and stir 3 minutes. Add fresh mushrooms and garlic; cook and stir 3 to 4 minutes. Add tomatoes with juice and red pepper flakes.

4. Drain porcini mushrooms; add liquid to skillet. If mushrooms are large, cut into ½-inch pieces; add to skillet. Bring to a boil over high heat. Reduce heat to medium; simmer, uncovered, 5 minutes or until slightly thickened. Stir in basil.

5. Spoon polenta onto 4 plates; top with mushroom mixture. Sprinkle with cheese.

makes 4 servings

Mushroom Ragoût with Polenta

Polenta Triangles

½ cup yellow corn grits
1½ cups chicken broth, divided
2 cloves garlic, minced
½ cup (2 ounces) crumbled feta cheese
1 red bell pepper, roasted, peeled and finely chopped

Combine grits and ½ cup chicken broth; mix well and set aside. Pour remaining 1 cup broth into large heavy saucepan; bring to a boil. Add garlic and moistened grits; mix well and return to a boil. Reduce heat to low; cover and cook 20 minutes. Remove from heat; add feta cheese. Stir until cheese is completely melted. Add pepper; mix well.

Spray 8-inch square pan with nonstick cooking spray. Spoon grits mixture into prepared pan. Press grits evenly into pan with wet fingertips. Refrigerate until cold.

Spray grid with nonstick cooking spray. Prepare grill for direct cooking. Turn polenta out onto cutting board and cut into 2-inch squares. Cut each square diagonally into 2 triangles.

Place polenta triangles on grid. Grill over medium-high heat 1 minute or until bottoms are lightly browned. Turn triangles over and grill until browned and crisp. Serve warm or at room temperature.

makes 8 servings

Tip

To roast pepper, place pepper on foil-lined broiler pan; broil 15 minutes or until blackened on all sides, turning every 5 minutes. Place pepper in a paper bag; close the bag and let the pepper stand 15 minutes before peeling. Some bits of charred skin will remain on pepper.

Polenta Triangles

Polenta with Pasta Sauce & Vegetables

    1 can (about 14 ounces) reduced-sodium chicken broth
1½ cups water
    1 cup yellow cornmeal
    2 teaspoons olive oil
12 ounces assorted cut vegetables, such as broccoli florets, bell peppers, red
        onions, zucchini squash and julienned carrots
    2 teaspoons fresh or bottled minced garlic
    2 cups prepared tomato-basil pasta sauce
    ½ cup grated Asiago cheese
    ¼ cup chopped fresh basil (optional)

1. To prepare polenta, whisk together chicken broth, water and cornmeal in large microwavable bowl. Cover with waxed paper; microwave at HIGH 5 minutes. Whisk well and microwave at HIGH 4 to 5 minutes more or until polenta is very thick. Whisk again; cover and keep warm.

2. Meanwhile, heat oil in a large deep nonstick skillet over medium heat. Add vegetables and garlic; cook and stir 5 minutes. Add pasta sauce; reduce heat, cover and simmer 5 to 8 minutes or until vegetables are tender.

3. Spoon polenta onto serving plates; top with pasta sauce mixture. Sprinkle with cheese and basil, if desired. *makes 4 servings*

prep time: 5 minutes
cook time: 15 minutes

Polenta with Pasta Sauce & Vegetables

Spinach Gnocchi

2 packages (10 ounces) frozen chopped spinach
1 cup ricotta cheese
2 eggs
⅔ cup freshly grated Parmesan cheese (about 2 ounces), divided
1 cup plus 3 tablespoons all-purpose flour, divided
½ teaspoon salt
⅛ teaspoon black pepper
⅛ teaspoon ground nutmeg
3 tablespoons butter or margarine, melted

1. Cook spinach according to package directions. Drain well; let cool. Squeeze spinach dry; place in medium bowl. Stir in ricotta cheese. Add eggs; mix well. Add ⅓ cup Parmesan cheese, 3 tablespoons flour, salt, pepper and nutmeg; mix. Cover; refrigerate 1 hour.

2. Spread remaining 1 cup flour in shallow baking pan. Press a heaping tablespoonful of spinach mixture between a spoon and your hand to form oval gnocchi; place on flour. Repeat with remaining spinach mixture.

3. Roll gnocchi lightly in flour to coat evenly; discard excess flour. Drop 8 to 12 gnocchi into large pot of boiling salted water; reduce heat to medium.

4. Cook, uncovered, 5 minutes or until gnocchi are slightly puffed and slightly firm to the touch. Remove gnocchi with slotted spoon; drain on paper towels. Immediately transfer to greased broilerproof shallow baking dish. Reheat water to boiling. Repeat with remaining gnocchi in batches of 8 to 12. Arrange gnocchi in single layer in baking dish.

5. Preheat broiler. Spoon butter over gnocchi; sprinkle with remaining ⅓ cup Parmesan cheese. Broil gnocchi 5 inches from heat 2 to 3 minutes until cheese melts and browns lightly. Serve immediately. Garnish as desired.   *makes 4 to 6 servings (about 24 gnocchi)*

Tomato-Artichoke Focaccia

    1 package (16 ounces) hot roll mix
    2 tablespoons wheat bran
1¼ cups hot water
    4 teaspoons olive oil, divided
    1 cup thinly sliced onions
    2 cloves garlic, minced
    4 ounces dry sun-dried tomatoes, rehydrated,* cut into strips
    1 cup canned artichoke hearts, sliced
    1 tablespoon minced fresh rosemary
    2 tablespoons freshly grated Parmesan cheese

To rehydrate sun-dried tomatoes, simply pour 1 cup boiling water over tomatoes in small heatproof bowl. Let tomatoes soak 5 to 10 minutes until softened; drain well.

1. Preheat oven to 400°F.

2. Combine dry ingredients and yeast packet from hot roll mix in large bowl. Add bran; mix well. Stir in hot water and 2 teaspoons oil. Knead dough about 5 minutes or until ingredients are blended.

3. Spray 15½×11½-inch baking pan or 14-inch pizza pan with nonstick cooking spray. Press dough onto bottom of prepared pan. Cover; let rise 15 minutes.

4. Heat 1 teaspoon oil in medium skillet over low heat. Add onions and garlic; cook and stir 2 to 3 minutes until onions are tender. Brush surface of dough with remaining 1 teaspoon oil. Top dough with onion mixture, tomatoes, artichokes and rosemary. Sprinkle with Parmesan.

5. Bake 25 to 30 minutes until lightly browned on top. To serve, cut into squares.

makes 16 servings

DESERTS

Lemon Raspberry Tiramisu

2 packages (8 ounces each) fat-free cream cheese, softened
6 packages artificial sweetener *or* equivalent of ¼ cup sugar
1 teaspoon vanilla
⅓ cup water
1 package (0.3 ounce) sugar-free lemon-flavored gelatin
2 cups thawed fat-free nondairy whipped topping
½ cup all-fruit red raspberry preserves
¼ cup water
2 tablespoons marsala wine
2 packages (3 ounces each) ladyfingers
1 pint fresh raspberries or frozen unsweetened raspberries, thawed

1. Combine cream cheese, artificial sweetener and vanilla in large bowl. Beat with electric mixer at high speed until smooth; set aside.

2. Combine water and gelatin in small microwavable bowl; microwave at HIGH 30 seconds to 1 minute or until water is boiling and gelatin is dissolved. Cool slightly.

3. Add gelatin mixture to cheese mixture; beat 1 minute. Add whipped topping; beat 1 minute more, scraping side of bowl. Set aside.

4. Whisk together preserves, water and marsala in small bowl until well blended. Reserve 2 tablespoons of preserves mixture; set aside. Spread ⅓ cup preserves mixture evenly over bottom of 11×7-inch glass baking dish.

5. Split ladyfingers in half; place half in bottom of baking dish. Spread half of cheese mixture evenly over ladyfingers; sprinkle 1 cup of raspberries evenly over cheese mixture. Top with remaining ladyfingers; spread remaining preserves mixture over ladyfingers. Top with remaining cheese mixture. Cover; refrigerate for at least 2 hours. Sprinkle with remaining raspberries and drizzle with reserved 2 tablespoons of preserves mixture before serving.

makes 12 servings

Lemon Raspberry Tiramisu

Caffé en Forchetta

2 cups reduced-fat (2%) milk
1 cup cholesterol-free egg substitute
½ cup sugar
2 tablespoons no-sugar-added mocha-flavored instant coffee
   Grated chocolate or 6 chocolate-covered coffee beans (optional)

1. Preheat oven to 325°F.

2. Combine all ingredients in medium bowl except grated chocolate. Whisk until instant coffee has dissolved and mixture is foamy. Pour into six individual custard cups. Place cups in 13×9-inch baking pan. Fill with hot water halfway up side of cups.

3. Bake 55 to 60 minutes or until knife inserted halfway between center and edge comes out clean. Serve warm or at room temperature. Garnish with grated chocolate or chocolate-covered coffee beans, if desired.   *makes 6 servings*

note: Enjoy your dinner coffee a whole new way. Translated from Italian, Caffé en Forchetta literally means "coffee on a fork." However, a spoon is recommended when serving this wonderfully creamy dessert.

Caffé en Forchetta

Tiramisu

2 packages (3 ounces each) ladyfingers, thawed if frozen, split in half horizontally
¾ cup brewed espresso*
2 tablespoons coffee liqueur or brandy (optional)
1 package (8 ounces) cream cheese, softened
2 tablespoons sugar
⅓ cup sour cream
½ cup whipping cream
2 tablespoons unsweetened cocoa powder, divided
Chocolate curls and mint leaves (optional)

*Use fresh brewed espresso, instant espresso powder prepared according to directions on jar or 2 teaspoons instant coffee powder dissolved in ¾ cup hot water.

Place ladyfingers on baking sheet, uncovered, 8 hours or overnight to dry. Or, dry ladyfingers by placing on microwavable plate. Microwave at MEDIUM-HIGH (70% power) 1 minute, turn ladyfingers over. Microwave at MEDIUM-HIGH 1 to 1½ minutes or just until dry.

Combine espresso and liqueur, if desired, in small bowl. Dip half the ladyfingers in espresso mixture; place in bottom of 2-quart serving bowl.

Beat cream cheese and sugar with electric mixer at medium speed until fluffy; add sour cream, beating until blended. Add whipping cream, beating until smooth. Spread half the cheese mixture over ladyfingers.

Place 1 tablespoon cocoa in fine strainer. Lightly tap rim of strainer and dust cocoa over cheese layer.

Dip remaining ladyfingers in espresso mixture. Place over cheese mixture in serving bowl.

Spread remaining cheese mixture over ladyfingers. Dust remaining 1 tablespoon cocoa over cheese layer. Refrigerate, covered, 4 hours or overnight. Garnish with chocolate curls and mint leaves, if desired.   *makes 6 servings*

Orange-Thyme Granita in Cookie Cups

2½ cups fresh orange juice
½ cup fresh lemon juice
¼ cup sugar
1 teaspoon finely chopped fresh thyme
6 Lemon Anise Cookie Cups (recipe follows)

Combine juices, sugar and thyme in medium bowl; stir until sugar dissolves. Freeze until slightly firm, about 1 hour. Beat with wire whisk to break ice crystals. Repeat freezing and beating process 2 to 3 times until ice is firm and granular.

Meanwhile, prepare Lemon Anise Cookie Cups. To serve, scoop ½ cup granita into each cookie cup.

makes 6 servings

Lemon Anise Cookie Cups

3 tablespoons all-purpose flour
3 tablespoons sugar
2 tablespoons margarine, melted
1 egg white
1 teaspoon grated lemon peel
¼ teaspoon anise extract
¼ cup sliced almonds

Preheat oven to 375°F. Combine flour, sugar, margarine, egg white, lemon peel and anise extract in food processor; process until smooth. Spray bottoms of 6 custard cups and 2 baking sheets with nonstick cooking spray. Spread 1 tablespoon batter into 5-inch-diameter circle on baking sheet with rubber spatula. Repeat to make total of 6 circles. Sprinkle 2 teaspoons almonds in center of each.

Bake 3 to 4 minutes or until edges are browned. Place each cookie over bottom of prepared custard cup so almonds face inside. Press cookies against custard cup to form cookie cup. Cool.

makes 6 cookie cups

Orange-Thyme Granita in Cookie Cup

Cannoli Pastries

    18 to 20 Cannoli Pastry Shells (recipe follows)
     2 pounds ricotta cheese
    1½ cups sifted powdered sugar
     2 teaspoons ground cinnamon
     ¼ cup diced candied orange peel, minced
     1 teaspoon grated lemon peel
        Powdered sugar
     2 ounces semisweet chocolate, finely chopped
        Orange peel strips and fresh mint leaves for garnish

1. Prepare Cannoli Pastry Shells; set aside.

2. For cannoli filling, beat cheese in large bowl with electric mixer at medium speed until smooth. Add 1½ cups powdered sugar and cinnamon; beat at high speed 3 minutes. Add candied orange peel and lemon peel; mix well. Cover and refrigerate until ready to serve.

3. To assemble, spoon cheese filling into pastry bag fitted with large plain tip. Pipe about ¼ cup filling into each reserved cannoli pastry shell.*

4. Roll Cannoli Pastries in additional powdered sugar to coat. Dip ends of pastries into chocolate. Arrange pastries on serving plate. Garnish, if desired.   *makes 18 to 20 pastries*

*Do not fill Cannoli Pastry Shells ahead of time or shells will become soggy.

Cannoli Pastry Shells

    1¾ cups all-purpose flour
     2 tablespoons granulated sugar
     1 teaspoon grated lemon peel
     2 tablespoons butter, cold
     1 egg
     6 tablespoons marsala
        Vegetable oil

continued on page 333

1. Mix flour, granulated sugar and lemon peel in medium bowl; cut in butter with 2 knives or pastry blender until mixture resembles fine crumbs. Beat egg and marsala in small bowl; add to flour mixture. Stir with fork to form ball. Divide dough in half; shape into two 1-inch-thick square pieces. Wrap in plastic wrap and refrigerate at least 1 hour.

2. Heat 1½ inches oil in large saucepan to 325°F. Working with 1 piece of dough at a time, roll out on lightly floured surface to ¹⁄₁₆-inch thickness. Cut dough into 9 or 10 (4×3-inch) rectangles.

3. Wrap each rectangle around a greased metal cannoli form or uncooked cannelloni pasta shell. Brush one edge of rectangle lightly with water; overlap with other edge and press firmly to seal.

4. Fry, 2 or 3 cannoli pastry shells at a time, 1 to 1½ minutes until light brown, turning once. Remove with tongs; drain on paper towels.

5. Cool until easy to handle. Carefully remove fried pastries from cannoli forms or pasta shells; cool completely. Repeat with remaining piece of dough.

makes 18 to 20 pastry shells

Tortoni

1½ cups cold half-and-half or milk
1 package (4-serving size) JELL-O® Pistachio Flavor Instant Pudding & Pie Filling
2 cups thawed COOL WHIP® Whipped Topping
½ cup chopped maraschino cherries
¼ cup BAKER'S® Semi-Sweet Real Chocolate Chips

POUR half-and-half into medium bowl. Add pudding mix. Beat with wire whisk 2 minutes. Gently stir in whipped topping, cherries and chips until blended. Spoon mixture into 10 paper-lined muffin cups.

FREEZE 3 hours or overnight.

makes 10 servings

Macédoine

Finely grated peel and juice of 1 lemon
Finely grated peel and juice of 1 lime
8 cups diced assorted seasonal fruits*
1 cup sweet spumante wine or freshly squeezed orange juice
¼ cup sugar
¼ cup coarsely chopped walnuts or almonds, toasted (optional)

Apples, pears and bananas are essential fruits in a traditional Macédoine. Add as many seasonally ripe fruits to them as you can—variety is the key. As you select fruits, try to achieve a diversity of textures, being sure to avoid mushy, overripe fruit.

1. Combine lemon juice and lime juice; place in large bowl. Place assorted fruits in bowl with citrus juice mixture; toss to coat.

2. Combine wine, sugar and citrus peels in 2-cup measuring cup, stirring until sugar is dissolved. Pour over fruit mixture; toss gently. Cover; refrigerate 1 hour.

3. Sprinkle walnuts on fruit mixture just before serving, if desired.   *makes 8 servings*

Apricot Rice Pudding

2 bags SUCCESS® Rice
2 cans (12 ounces *each*) evaporated skim milk, divided
1 cup sugar
3 egg whites
1½ teaspoons vanilla
1 can (16 ounces) apricots, drained and chopped

Prepare rice according to package directions.

Combine rice, 2 cups milk and sugar in medium saucepan. Cook over medium heat until thick and creamy, about 20 minutes, stirring constantly.

Beat egg whites with remaining 1 cup milk in medium bowl until well blended. Add to rice mixture. Reduce heat to low; simmer, stirring constantly, until thickened, 3 to 4 minutes. Blend in vanilla. Gently stir in apricots. Cool. Serve warm or chilled.   *makes 8 servings*

Macédoine

Creamy Cappuccino Frozen Dessert

DESSERT
  1 package (8 ounces) cream cheese, softened
  1 can (14 ounces) sweetened condensed milk
  ½ cup chocolate-flavored syrup
  1 tablespoon instant coffee powder
  1 tablespoon hot water
  1½ cups frozen whipped topping, thawed
  1 prepared chocolate crumb crust (6 ounces)
  ¼ cup chopped pecans, toasted

TOPPING
  Additional chocolate-flavored syrup

1. For dessert, beat cream cheese in large mixing bowl on medium speed of electric mixer for 2 to 3 minutes or until fluffy. Add sweetened condensed milk and ½ cup syrup; beat on low speed until well blended.

2. Dissolve coffee powder in hot water in small bowl. Slowly stir into cream cheese mixture. Fold in whipped topping; spoon mixture into crust. Sprinkle with pecans. Cover and freeze overnight.

3. To complete recipe, let dessert stand in refrigerator 10 to 15 minutes before serving. Cut into wedges. For topping, drizzle with additional syrup.   *makes 16 servings*

make-ahead time: 1 day or up to 1 week before serving
final prep/stand time: 15 minutes

Creamy Cappuccino Frozen Dessert

Cherry Rice Pudding

   1½ cups milk
    1 cup cooked, converted or long-grain rice
    3 eggs, beaten
   ½ cup sugar
   ½ teaspoon almond extract
   ¼ teaspoon salt
   ¼ cup dried cherries or cranberries

Combine all ingredients in large bowl. Pour mixture into greased 1½-quart casserole. Cover with foil. Add rack to 5-quart slow cooker and pour in 1 cup water. Place casserole on rack. Cover and cook on LOW 4 hours. Remove casserole from slow cooker. Let stand 15 minutes before serving.

makes 6 servings

Chocolate Tortoni

    8 squares (1 ounce each) semi-sweet chocolate
   ⅔ cup KARO® Light or Dark Corn Syrup
    2 cups heavy cream, divided
   1½ cups broken chocolate wafer cookies
    1 cup coarsely chopped walnuts
     Chocolate, nuts and whipped cream (optional)

1. Line 12 (2½-inch) muffin pan cups with paper or foil liners.

2. In large heavy saucepan combine chocolate and corn syrup; stir over low heat just until chocolate melts. Remove from heat. Stir in ½ cup cream until blended.

3. Refrigerate 25 to 30 minutes or until cool. Stir in cookies and walnuts.

4. In small bowl with mixer at medium speed, beat remaining 1½ cups cream until soft peaks form; gently fold into chocolate mixture just until combined. Spoon into prepared muffin pan cups.

5. Freeze 4 hours or until firm. Let stand at room temperature several minutes before serving. If desired, garnish with chocolate, nuts or whipped cream. Store covered in freezer for up to 1 month.

makes 12 servings

prep time: 15 minutes, plus chilling and freezing

Tiramisu

⅓ cup GENERAL FOODS INTERNATIONAL COFFEES, Sugar Free Fat Free
    Suisse Mocha Flavor, divided
2 tablespoons hot water
1 package (3 ounces) ladyfingers, split
2½ cups cold fat-free milk, divided
1 container (8 ounces) PHILADELPHIA FREE® Soft Fat Free Cream Cheese
2 packages (4-serving size each) JELL-O® Vanilla Flavor Fat Free Sugar Free
    Instant Reduced Calorie Pudding & Pie Filling
1 cup thawed COOL WHIP LITE® Whipped Topping

DISSOLVE 1 tablespoon of the flavored instant coffee in hot water in small bowl.

COVER bottom and sides of shallow 2-quart dessert dish with ladyfingers. Sprinkle dissolved flavored instant coffee over ladyfingers.

PLACE ½ cup of the milk, cream cheese and remaining undissolved flavored instant coffee in blender container; cover. Blend on medium speed until smooth. Add pudding mixes and remaining 2 cups milk; cover. Blend on medium speed until smooth. Carefully pour into prepared bowl. Top with whipped topping.

REFRIGERATE at least 3 hours or until set. Just before serving, sprinkle with additional undissolved flavored instant coffee, if desired. *makes 12 servings*

prep: 15 minutes plus refrigerating

Tip

Ladyfingers are light, delicate finger-shaped sponge cakes. They can be purchased in bakeries or supermarkets.

Italian Ice

1 cup sweet or dry fruity white wine
1 cup water
1 cup sugar
1 cup lemon juice
2 egg whites*
  Fresh berries (optional)
  Mint leaves for garnish

Use clean, uncracked eggs.

1. Place wine and water in small saucepan; add sugar. Cook over medium-high heat until sugar has dissolved and syrup boils, stirring frequently. Cover; boil 1 minute. Uncover; adjust heat to maintain simmer. Simmer 10 minutes without stirring. Remove from heat. Refrigerate 1 hour or until syrup is completely cool.

2. Stir lemon juice into cooled syrup. Pour into 9-inch round cake pan. Freeze 1 hour.

3. Quickly stir mixture with fork breaking up ice crystals. Freeze 1 hour more or until firm but not solid. Meanwhile, place medium bowl in freezer to chill.

4. Beat egg whites in small bowl with electric mixer at high speed until stiff peaks form. Remove lemon ice mixture from cake pan to chilled bowl. Immediately beat ice with whisk or fork until smooth. Fold in egg whites; mix well. Spread egg mixture evenly into same cake pan. Freeze 30 minutes. Immediately stir with fork; cover cake pan with foil. Freeze at least 3 hours or until firm.

5. To serve, scoop Italian Ice into fluted champagne glasses or dessert dishes. Serve with berries. Garnish, if desired.   *makes 4 servings*

Custard Rum Torte

        6 eggs
1¼ cups granulated sugar, divided
   ¾ teaspoon salt, divided
1¼ cups all-purpose flour
   ⅓ cup cornstarch
3½ cups milk
      2 egg yolks
      2 tablespoons butter
      2 teaspoons vanilla extract
      2 pints fresh strawberries
      6 tablespoons dark rum
      4 cups heavy or whipping cream (2 pints)
   ¼ cup powdered sugar, sifted

1. For cake, preheat oven to 350°F. Grease and flour 10-inch springform pan. Beat eggs in large bowl with electric mixer at high speed until foamy. Beat in ¾ cup granulated sugar, 2 tablespoons at a time, beating well after each addition. Beat 3 minutes more. Beat in ¼ teaspoon salt. Sift ⅓ of flour over egg mixture; fold in. Repeat until all flour has been incorporated.

2. Spread batter into prepared pan. Bake 40 minutes or until toothpick inserted in center comes out clean. Cool in pan on wire rack 10 minutes. Loosen cake from side of pan; remove side of pan. Remove cake from bottom of pan to wire rack. Cool completely. Clean pan.

3. For custard, combine remaining ½ cup granulated sugar, cornstarch and remaining ½ teaspoon salt in large saucepan; mix well. Stir in milk until smooth. Bring to a boil over medium heat, stirring frequently. Boil 3 minutes, stirring constantly; remove from heat. Whisk egg yolks in small bowl; gradually whisk in 1 cup hot milk mixture. Gradually whisk egg yolk mixture into remaining milk mixture in saucepan. Cook over low heat 1 minute, stirring constantly. Immediately pour custard into medium bowl. Cut butter into 6 pieces; add to custard and stir until melted. Stir in vanilla extract. Press waxed paper onto surface of custard; refrigerate. Cool completely.

continued on page 344
Custard Rum Torte

Custard Rum Torte, continued

4. Reserve 8 whole strawberries for garnish. Hull and thinly slice remaining strawberries.

5. Cut cake horizontally into 3 even layers using thin serrated knife. To assemble torte, brush top of each cake layer with 2 tablespoons rum. Place one cake layer in bottom of springform pan. Spread with ½ of custard. Arrange ½ of strawberry slices over custard in single layer. Top with second cake layer; spread with remaining custard and top with remaining strawberry slices. Place third cake layer on top. Cover and refrigerate at least 12 hours.

6. About 45 minutes before serving, beat cream with powdered sugar in large bowl with electric mixer at high speed until stiff. Spoon 2 cups whipped cream mixture into pastry bag fitted with large star tip; refrigerate. Remove side of pan; place dessert on serving plate (do not remove bottom of pan). Spread remaining whipped cream mixture on sides and top of torte. Pipe reserved whipped cream mixture around top and bottom edges. Refrigerate 30 minutes before serving. To serve, garnish with reserved whole strawberries. Cut torte into slices. Refrigerate leftovers.
makes 10 to 12 servings

Italian Cheese Pie

    1 cup ricotta cheese
    ¾ cup cold milk
    1½ teaspoons grated orange peel
    1 package (4-serving size) JELL-O® White Chocolate *or* Vanilla Flavor Instant Pudding & Pie Filling
    1 tub (8 ounces) COOL WHIP® Whipped Topping, thawed
    ½ cup plus 2 tablespoons BAKER'S® Semi-Sweet Real Chocolate Chips
    1 prepared shortbread crumb crust (6 ounces *or* 9 inches)
    Orange slices

BEAT ricotta cheese, milk and orange peel in large bowl with wire whisk until blended. Add pudding mix. Beat with wire whisk 1 to 2 minutes. Gently stir in 2 cups whipped topping and ½ cup chocolate chips. Spoon into crust.

REFRIGERATE 2 hours or until firm. Garnish with remaining whipped topping, remaining 2 tablespoons chocolate chips and orange slices.
makes 8 servings

prep time: 10 minutes

Fig and Hazelnut Cake

¾ cup hazelnuts or filberts, skins removed and coarsely chopped
¾ cup whole dried figs (about 4 ounces), coarsely chopped
⅔ cup slivered blanched almonds (about 3 ounces), coarsely chopped
3 ounces semisweet chocolate, finely chopped
⅓ cup diced candied orange peel
⅓ cup diced candied lemon peel
3 eggs
½ cup sugar
1¼ cups all-purpose flour
1¾ teaspoons baking powder
¾ teaspoon salt

1. Preheat oven to 300°F. Grease 8×4-inch loaf pan. Combine hazelnuts, figs, almonds, chocolate, candied orange and lemon peels in medium bowl; mix well.

2. Beat eggs and sugar in large bowl with electric mixer at high speed at least 5 minutes or until mixture is pale yellow and thick and fluffy. Gently fold nut mixture into egg mixture.

3. Combine flour, baking powder and salt in small bowl. Sift ½ of flour mixture over nut-egg mixture and gently fold in; repeat with remaining flour mixture.

4. Spread batter evenly into prepared pan. Bake 60 to 70 minutes until top is deep golden brown and firm to the touch. Cool in pan on wire rack 5 minutes. Remove loaf from pan; cool completely on wire rack at least 4 hours. Slice and serve.   *makes 12 to 16 servings*

Tip

Hazelnuts, also known as filberts, have thin brown, bitter skins that are best removed before eating. To remove the skins, place the nuts on a baking sheet and bake them in a preheated 350°F oven for 7 to 10 minutes or until the skins begin to flake off. Remove them from the oven, wrap them in a heavy towel and rub them against the towel to remove as much of the skins as possible.

Espresso Swirl Cheesecake

  1 package (9 ounces) chocolate wafer cookies
  1 tablespoon plus 1½ cups sugar
  6 tablespoons I CAN'T BELIEVE IT'S NOT BUTTER!® Spread
  3 tablespoons instant espresso coffee powder, divided
  4 packages (8 ounces each) cream cheese, softened
  ⅓ cup all-purpose flour
  ½ cup (1 stick) I CAN'T BELIEVE IT'S NOT BUTTER!® Spread, melted
  7 eggs, slightly beaten
  1 cup (½ pint) whipping or heavy cream
  2 teaspoons vanilla extract
  2 squares (1 ounce each) bittersweet chocolate *or* ⅓ cup semi-sweet chocolate
    chips

On bottom rack in oven, place 13×9-inch pan filled halfway with water. Preheat oven to 350°F.

In food processor, process cookies and 1 tablespoon sugar until combined; set aside. In small saucepan, melt 6 tablespoons I Can't Believe It's Not Butter! Spread, then stir in 1 tablespoon instant coffee until dissolved. Remove from heat; stir in cookie mixture. In 9-inch springform pan, press crumb mixture onto bottom and up sides.

In medium bowl, with electric mixer, beat cream cheese, remaining 1½ cups sugar, flour and melted ½ cup I Can't Believe It's Not Butter! Spread 2 minutes or until mixture is creamy. Gradually beat in eggs, cream and vanilla until smooth. Reserve 1 cup batter. Pour remaining batter into prepared pan.

In microwave-safe bowl, microwave chocolate at HIGH (Full Power) 1 minute or until chocolate is melted; stir until smooth. Stir in remaining 2 tablespoons instant coffee until dissolved. Stir chocolate mixture into reserved batter until blended. Drop mixture by 2 tablespoonfuls onto batter and swirl with knife.

Bake 1 hour 10 minutes or until edges are golden. Without opening the door, turn oven off and let cheesecake stand in oven 30 minutes. On wire rack, cool completely. Cover and refrigerate overnight. Best if made 1 day ahead.   *makes 12 servings*

Espresso Swirl Cheesecake

Rum and Spumone Layered Torte

  1 package (18 to 19 ounces) moist butter recipe yellow cake mix
  3 eggs
  ½ cup butter, softened
  ⅓ cup plus 2 teaspoons rum, divided
  ⅓ cup water
  1 quart spumone ice cream, softened
  1 cup whipping cream
  1 tablespoon powdered sugar
    Chopped mixed candied fruit
    Red and green sugars for decorating (optional)

Preheat oven to 375°F. Grease and flour 15½×10½×1-inch jelly-roll pan. Combine cake mix, eggs, butter, ⅓ cup rum and water in large bowl. Beat with electric mixer at low speed until moistened. Beat at high speed 4 minutes. Pour evenly into prepared pan.

Bake 20 to 25 minutes or until toothpick inserted in center comes out clean. Cool in pan 10 minutes. Turn out of pan onto wire rack; cool completely.

Cut cake into three 10×5-inch pieces. Place one cake layer on serving plate. Spread with half the softened ice cream. Cover with second cake layer. Spread with remaining ice cream. Place remaining cake layer on top. Gently push down. Wrap cake in plastic wrap and freeze at least 4 hours.

Just before serving, combine cream, powdered sugar and remaining 2 teaspoons rum in small chilled bowl. Beat at high speed with chilled beaters until stiff peaks form. Remove cake from freezer. Spread thin layer of whipped cream mixture over top of cake. Place star tip in pastry bag; fill with remaining whipped cream mixture. Pipe rosettes around outer top edges of cake. Place candied fruit in narrow strip down center of cake. Sprinkle colored sugars over rosettes, if desired. Serve immediately. *makes 8 to 10 servings*

Rum and Spumone Layered Torte

Chocolate Espresso Cake

          2 cups cake flour
      1½ teaspoons baking soda
        ½ teaspoon salt
        ½ cup butter, softened
          1 cup granulated sugar
          1 cup packed light brown sugar
          3 eggs
          4 squares (1 ounce each) unsweetened chocolate, melted
        ¾ cup sour cream
          1 teaspoon vanilla
          1 cup brewed espresso*
            Creamy Chocolate Frosting (recipe page 352)
            White Chocolate Curls (recipe page 352, optional)

*Use fresh brewed espresso, instant espresso powder prepared according to directions on jar or 1 tablespoon instant coffee powder dissolved in 1 cup hot water.

Preheat oven to 350°F. Line bottoms of two 9-inch round cake pans with waxed paper; lightly grease paper. Combine flour, baking soda and salt in medium bowl; set aside.

Beat butter and sugars in large bowl with electric mixer at medium speed until light and fluffy. Add eggs, one at a time, beating well after each addition. Add melted chocolate, sour cream and vanilla; beat until blended. Add flour mixture alternately with espresso, beating well after each addition. Pour batter evenly into prepared pans.

Bake 35 minutes or until wooden pick inserted into center comes out clean. Cool layers in pans on wire rack 10 minutes. Loosen edges and invert layers onto rack to cool completely.

Prepare Creamy Chocolate Frosting and White Chocolate Curls, if desired. To fill and frost cake, place one layer on cake plate; frost top with Creamy Chocolate Frosting. Place second layer over frosting. Frost top and side with frosting; smooth frosting. Place White Chocolate Curls on cake, if desired. *makes 12 servings*

continued on page 352

Chocolate Espresso Cake

Creamy Chocolate Frosting

½ cup butter or margarine, softened
4 cups powdered sugar
5 to 6 tablespoons brewed espresso, divided
½ cup (3 ounces) semisweet chocolate chips, melted
1 teaspoon vanilla
  Dash salt
2 squares (1 ounce each) white chocolate

Beat butter in large bowl with electric mixer at medium speed until creamy. Gradually add powdered sugar and 4 tablespoons espresso; beat until smooth. Beat in melted chocolate, vanilla and salt. Add remaining espresso, 1 tablespoon at a time, until frosting is desired spreading consistency.

White Chocolate Curls: Pull vegetable peeler across 2 squares (1 ounce each) room temperature white chocolate to create curls. Carefully pick up each chocolate curl by inserting a toothpick into center of the curl. Place on waxed paper-lined baking sheet. Refrigerate 15 minutes or until firm.

Raspberry Tortoni Cake Roll

Raspberry Tortoni Filling (recipe page 354)
3 eggs, separated
¾ cup granulated sugar
¼ cup skim milk
1 teaspoon vanilla
¾ cup all-purpose flour
1½ teaspoons baking powder
¼ teaspoon salt
¼ teaspoon cream of tartar
Powdered sugar
¼ cup fresh raspberries (optional)
Mint sprigs (optional)

1. Prepare Raspberry Tortoni Filling. Set aside.

2. Lightly grease 15×10×1-inch jelly-roll pan and line with waxed paper; lightly grease and flour paper. Preheat oven to 400°F. Beat egg yolks in medium bowl with electric mixer at high speed 1 minute; gradually beat in granulated sugar until yolks are thick and lemon colored, about 5 minutes. Beat in milk and vanilla; mix in flour, baking powder and salt.

3. Beat egg whites in medium bowl at high speed until foamy; add cream of tartar and beat until stiff peaks form. Fold about one-third egg white mixture into cake batter; gently fold cake batter into remaining egg white mixture. Spread batter evenly in prepared pan.

4. Bake 8 to 10 minutes or until cake begins to brown. Immediately invert onto clean towel that has been sprinkled with 1 tablespoon powdered sugar. Peel off waxed paper; roll cake up in towel and cool on wire rack only 10 minutes.

5. Gently unroll cake and spread with Raspberry Tortoni Filling. Roll cake up; wrap in plastic wrap or foil and freeze until firm, at least 8 hours or overnight.

6. Remove cake from freezer; unwrap and trim ends, if uneven. Place cake on serving plate. Sprinkle with additional powdered sugar, fresh raspberries and mint, if desired.

makes 12 servings

continued on page 354

Raspberry Tortoni Filling

2 cups fresh or frozen unsweetened raspberries, thawed, drained and divided
1 tablespoon sugar
2 envelopes (1.3 ounces each) whipped topping mix
1 cup 1% lowfat milk
½ teaspoon rum or sherry extract (optional)
¼ cup pistachio nuts or coarsely chopped blanched almonds

1. Place 1 cup raspberries in food processor or blender; process until smooth. Strain and discard seeds. Sprinkle sugar over remaining 1 cup raspberries.

2. Beat whipped topping mix with milk in medium bowl at high speed until stiff peaks form; fold in raspberry purée and rum, if desired. Fold in sugared raspberries and nuts.

makes 4 cups

Tip

Pistachio nuts have a hard tan shell which is sometimes dyed pink or blanched until white. They are grown in California, Iran, Italy and Turkey. The inside meat has a pale green color and a delicate, subtly sweet flavor.

Raspberry Tortoni Cake Roll

Italian Ricotta Torte

8 eggs, separated
1½ cups sugar, divided
1½ cups ground blanched almonds
⅔ cup all-purpose flour
⅔ cup HERSHEY'S Cocoa
1 teaspoon baking soda
½ teaspoon salt
½ cup water
2 teaspoons vanilla extract
½ teaspoon almond extract
Cocoa Whipped Cream (recipe page 358)
Ricotta Cherry Filling (recipe page 358)

1. Heat oven to 375°F. Grease bottoms of two 9-inch round baking pans; line with wax paper. Grease wax paper lining leaving sides of pans ungreased.

2. Beat egg yolks in large bowl on medium speed of mixer 3 minutes. Gradually add 1 cup sugar, beating another 2 minutes. Stir together almonds, flour, cocoa, baking soda and salt; add alternately with water to egg yolk mixture, beating on low speed just until blended. Stir in vanilla and almond extract.

3. Beat egg whites in large bowl until foamy. Gradually add remaining ½ cup sugar, beating until stiff peaks form. Carefully fold chocolate mixture into beaten egg whites. Spread batter evenly into prepared pans.

4. Bake 20 to 22 minutes or until top springs back when touched lightly. Cool 10 minutes; remove from pans to wire racks. Cool completely. With long serrated knife, cut each layer in half horizontally to make 4 thin layers. Refrigerate layers while preparing filling and whipped cream.

5. Place one cake layer on plate; spread with ⅓ (about 1⅓ cups) Ricotta Cherry Filling. Top with another cake layer. Repeat with remaining filling and layers. Frost sides and top with Cocoa Whipped Cream. Garnish with candied cherries or sliced almonds, if desired. Refrigerate at least 4 hours. Cover; refrigerate leftover torte.   *makes 8 to 10 servings*

continued on page 358

Italian Ricotta Torte

Cocoa Whipped Cream: Stir together ⅔ cup powdered sugar and ⅓ cup HERSHEY'S Cocoa in large bowl. Add 2 cups (1 pint) cold whipping cream and 2 teaspoons vanilla extract; beat just until stiff. (Do not overbeat.)

Ricotta Cherry Filling

  1 cup (½ pint) cold whipping cream
1¾ cups (15 ounces) ricotta cheese
  ⅓ cup powdered sugar
  ½ cup chopped candied cherries
  ½ teaspoon almond extract

1. Beat whipping cream in small bowl until stiff. Beat ricotta cheese and powdered sugar in large bowl until smooth. Fold whipping cream into cheese mixture just until blended. Stir in candied cherries and almond extract. *makes about 4 cups*

prep time: 40 minutes
bake time: 20 minutes
cool time: 1 hour
chill time: 4 hours

Lemon Cream Almond Torte

TORTE
½ cup sifted cake flour
½ teaspoon baking powder
⅛ teaspoon salt
½ cup softened butter
¾ cup granulated sugar
1 cup BLUE DIAMOND® Blanched Almond Paste
3 eggs
1 tablespoon brandy
1 teaspoon vanilla extract
⅛ teaspoon almond extract

LEMON CREAM
3 egg yolks
⅓ cup granulated sugar
2 tablespoons flour
1 cup milk, scalded
2 teaspoons grated lemon peel
2 tablespoons lemon juice
½ teaspoon vanilla extract

GARNISH
Powdered sugar

Sift together flour, baking powder and salt; set aside. Cream butter and sugar. Add almond paste and beat until mixture is smooth. Add eggs one at a time, beating well after each addition. Mix in brandy, vanilla and almond extract. On lowest speed, add flour mixture. Pour into a greased and floured 8-inch round cake pan (at least 2 inches deep) or springform pan. Bake at 325°F. for 45 minutes or until a toothpick inserted in center comes out clean. Cool in pan 15 minutes. Remove and cool right-side up on wire rack. Meanwhile, prepare Lemon Cream. Beat yolks and sugar until mixture is thick and pale yellow. Stir in flour. Gradually pour hot milk into egg mixture, whisking constantly. Stir in grated lemon peel. Boil mixture 1 minute, whisking constantly. Remove from heat, add lemon juice and vanilla; stir until cooled. Slice cake into 2 layers. Spread Lemon Cream over bottom layer; top with second layer. Place a lace doily over top of torte. Sift powdered sugar evenly over top and carefully remove doily. Chill. *makes 8 to 10 servings*

Florentine Cookies

¼ cup unsalted butter
¼ cup sugar
 1 tablespoon heavy or whipping cream
¼ cup sliced blanched almonds, finely chopped
¼ cup walnuts, finely chopped
 5 red candied cherries, finely chopped
 1 tablespoon golden or dark raisins, finely chopped
 1 tablespoon crystallized ginger, finely chopped
 1 tablespoon diced candied lemon peel, finely chopped
 3 tablespoons all-purpose flour
 4 ounces semisweet chocolate, chopped

1. Preheat oven to 350°F. Grease 2 large baking sheets.

2. Combine butter, sugar and cream in small, heavy saucepan. Cook, uncovered, over medium heat until sugar dissolves and mixture boils, stirring constantly. Cook and stir 1 minute; remove from heat. Stir in nuts, candied cherries, raisins, ginger and candied lemon peel. Add flour; mix well.

3. Spoon heaping teaspoon batter onto prepared baking sheet. Repeat, placing 4 cookies on each baking sheet to allow room for spreading.

4. Bake cookies, 1 baking sheet at a time, 8 to 10 minutes until deep brown. Remove baking sheet from oven to wire rack. (If cookies have spread unevenly, push in edges with metal spatula to round out shape.) Cool cookies 1 minute or until firm enough to remove from sheet, then quickly but carefully remove cookies to wire racks. Cool completely.

5. Repeat with remaining batter. (To prevent cookies from spreading too quickly, allow baking sheets to cool before greasing and spooning batter onto sheets.)

6. Bring water in bottom of double boiler just to a boil; remove from heat. Place chocolate in top of double boiler and place over water. Stir chocolate until melted; immediately remove from water. Let chocolate cool slightly.

7. Line large baking sheet with waxed paper. Turn cookies over; spread chocolate on bottoms. Place cookies, chocolate side up, on prepared baking sheet; let stand until chocolate is almost set. Score chocolate in zig-zag pattern with tines of fork. Refrigerate until firm. Serve or store in airtight container in refrigerator. *makes about 2 dozen cookies*

Florentine Cookies

Fruit & Nut Biscotti Toasts

       2 cups all-purpose flour
     ¾ cup sugar
     ½ cup cornmeal
     ½ cups finely chopped toasted walnuts
    1½ teaspoon baking powder
     ½ teaspoon baking soda
     ¾ cup I CAN'T BELIEVE IT'S NOT BUTTER!® Spread, melted and cooled
       3 eggs
    1½ teaspoon vanilla extract
     ½ cup finely chopped citron (optional)
     ¼ cup dried cranberries or raisins

Preheat oven to 325°F.

In large bowl, combine flour, sugar, cornmeal, walnuts, baking powder and baking soda; set aside.

In small bowl, with wire whisk, beat I Can't Believe It's Not Butter! Spread, eggs and vanilla. Add to flour mixture, stirring until mixture forms a dough. Stir in citron and cranberries. Chill 1 hour.

On lightly floured surface, knead dough. Divide in half. On greased baking sheet, with floured hands, shape dough into two flat logs, about 14×1½-inches each. Bake 30 minutes or until firm. On wire rack, cool 10 minutes.

On cutting board, cut logs into ½-inch-thick diagonal slices. On baking sheet, arrange cookies cut side down. Bake an additional 20 minutes, turning once. On wire rack, cool completely. Store in airtight container.   *makes about 2½ dozen toasts*

Cappuccino Bon Bons

1 package DUNCAN HINES® Chocolate Lovers Chewy Fudge Brownie Mix
2 eggs
⅓ cup water
⅓ cup vegetable oil
1½ tablespoons instant coffee
1 teaspoon ground cinnamon
Whipped topping
Cinnamon

1. Preheat oven to 350°F. Place 40 (2-inch) foil cupcake liners on cookie sheet.

2. Combine brownie mix, eggs, water, oil, instant coffee and cinnamon. Stir with spoon until well blended, about 50 strokes. Fill each cupcake liner with 1 measuring tablespoonful batter. Bake at 350°F for 12 to 15 minutes or until toothpick inserted in center comes out clean. Cool completely. Garnish with whipped topping and a dash of cinnamon. Refrigerate until ready to serve. *makes 40 bon bons*

Classic Anise Biscotti

    4 ounces whole blanched almonds (about ¾ cup)
2¼ cups all-purpose flour
    1 teaspoon baking powder
    ¾ teaspoon salt
    ¾ cup sugar
    ½ cup unsalted butter, softened
    3 eggs
    2 tablespoons brandy
    2 teaspoons grated lemon peel
    1 tablespoon whole anise seeds

1. Preheat oven to 375°F. To toast almonds, spread almonds on baking sheet. Bake 6 to 8 minutes until toasted and light brown; turn off oven. Remove almonds with spoon to cutting board; cool. Coarsely chop almonds.

2. Combine flour, baking powder and salt in small bowl. Beat sugar and butter in medium bowl with electric mixer at medium speed until light and fluffy. Add eggs, 1 at a time, beating well after each addition and scraping sides of bowl often. Stir in brandy and lemon peel. Add flour mixture gradually; stir until smooth. Stir in almonds and anise seeds. Cover and refrigerate dough 1 hour or until firm.

3. Preheat oven to 375°F. Grease large baking sheet. Divide dough in half. Shape ½ of dough into 12×2-inch log on lightly floured surface. (Dough will be fairly soft.) Pat smooth with lightly floured fingertips. Repeat with remaining ½ of dough to form second log. Bake 20 to 25 minutes until logs are light golden brown. Remove baking sheet from oven to wire rack; turn off oven. Cool logs completely.

4. Preheat oven to 350°F. Cut logs diagonally with serrated knife into ½-inch-thick slices. Place slices flat in single layer on 2 ungreased baking sheets.

5. Bake 8 minutes. Turn slices over; bake 10 to 12 minutes more until cut surfaces are light brown and cookies are dry. Remove cookies to wire racks; cool completely. Store cookies in airtight container up to 2 weeks.   *makes about 4 dozen cookies*

Classic Anise Biscotti

Chocolate Almond Biscotti

2 cups (12-ounce package) NESTLÉ® TOLL HOUSE® Semi-Sweet Chocolate
    Morsels, divided
2 cups all-purpose flour
¼ cup NESTLÉ® TOLL HOUSE® Baking Cocoa
1½ teaspoons baking powder
¼ teaspoon baking soda
¼ teaspoon salt
½ cup granulated sugar
½ cup packed brown sugar
¼ cup (½ stick) butter or margarine, softened
½ teaspoon vanilla extract
½ teaspoon almond extract
3 eggs
1 cup slivered almonds, toasted
Chocolate Coating (optional, recipe page 367)

MICROWAVE 1 cup morsels in small, microwave-safe bowl on HIGH (100%) power for 1 minute; stir. Microwave at additional 10- to 20-second intervals, stirring until smooth; cool to room temperature. Combine flour, cocoa, baking powder, baking soda and salt in medium bowl.

BEAT granulated sugar, brown sugar, butter, vanilla and almond extracts until crumbly. Add eggs one at a time, beating well after each addition. Beat in melted chocolate. Gradually beat in flour mixture. Stir in nuts. Chill for 15 minutes or until firm.

SHAPE dough into two (3-inch-wide by 1-inch-high) loaves with floured hands on 1 large or 2 small greased baking sheets.

continued on page 367

BAKE in preheated 325°F. oven for 40 to 50 minutes or until firm. Cool on baking sheets for 15 minutes. Cut into ¾-inch-thick slices; turn slices onto their sides. Bake for 10 minutes on each side until dry. Remove to wire racks to cool completely.

For Chocolate Coating: MICROWAVE *remaining* morsels and 2 tablespoons shortening in medium, microwave-safe bowl on HIGH (100%) power for 1 minute; stir. Microwave at 10- to 20-second intervals, stirring until smooth. Dip biscotti halfway into chocolate coating, pushing mixture up with a spatula; shake off excess. Place on waxed paper-lined tray. Chill for 10 minutes or until chocolate is set. Store in airtight containers in cool place or in refrigerator.   *makes about 2½ dozen cookies*

Creamy Cappuccino Brownies

    1 package (21 to 24 ounces) brownie mix
    1 tablespoon coffee crystals *or* 1 teaspoon espresso powder
    2 tablespoons warm water
    1 cup (8 ounces) Wisconsin Mascarpone cheese
    3 tablespoons sugar
    1 egg
      Powdered sugar

Grease bottom of 13×9-inch baking pan. Prepare brownie mix according to package directions. Pour half of batter into prepared pan. Dissolve coffee crystals in water; add Mascarpone, sugar and egg. Blend until smooth. Drop by spoonfuls over brownie batter; top with remaining brownie batter. With knife, swirl cheese mixture through brownies creating a marbled effect. Bake at 375°F 30 to 35 minutes or until toothpick inserted in center comes out clean. Sprinkle with powdered sugar.   *makes 2 dozen brownies*

Favorite recipe from **Wisconsin Milk Marketing Board**

Mocha Biscotti

2½ cups all-purpose flour
½ cup unsweetened cocoa
2 teaspoons DAVIS® Baking Powder
1¼ cups sugar
¾ cup egg substitute
¼ cup margarine or butter, melted
4 teaspoons instant coffee powder
½ teaspoon vanilla extract
⅓ cup PLANTERS® Slivered Almonds, chopped
Powdered sugar, optional

1. Mix flour, cocoa and baking powder in small bowl; set aside.

2. Beat sugar, egg substitute, melted margarine or butter, coffee powder and vanilla in large bowl with mixer at medium speed for 2 minutes. Stir in flour mixture and almonds.

3. Divide dough in half. Shape each portion of dough with floured hands into 14×2-inch log on a greased baking sheet. (Dough will be sticky). Bake in preheated 350°F oven for 25 minutes.

4. Remove from oven and cut each log on a diagonal into 16 (1-inch) slices. Place biscotti, cut-side up, on baking sheets; return to oven and bake 10 to 15 minutes more on each side or until lightly toasted.

5. Remove from sheets. Cool completely on wire racks. Dust biscotti tops with powdered sugar if desired. Store in airtight container.   *makes 32 biscotti*

preparation time: 20 minutes
cook time: 35 minutes
total time: 1 hour and 5 minutes

Mocha Biscotti

Spumone Bars

¾ cup butter, softened
⅔ cup sugar
3 egg yolks
1 teaspoon vanilla
¼ teaspoon baking powder
⅛ teaspoon salt
2 cups all-purpose flour
12 maraschino cherries, well drained and chopped
¼ cup chopped walnuts
¼ cup mint-flavored or plain semisweet chocolate chips
2 teaspoons water, divided

Preheat oven to 350°F. Cream butter and sugar in large bowl until blended. Beat in egg yolks, vanilla, baking powder and salt until light. Stir in flour to make a stiff dough. Divide dough into 3 equal parts; place each part in small bowl. Add cherries and walnuts to one part, blending well. Melt chocolate chips in small bowl over hot water. Stir until smooth. Add melted chocolate and 1 teaspoon of the water to second part, blending well. Stir remaining 1 teaspoon water into third part. (If doughs are soft, refrigerate 10 minutes.)

Divide each color dough into 4 equal parts. Shape each part into a 6-inch rope by rolling on lightly floured surface. Place one rope of each color side by side on ungreased cookie sheet. Flatten ropes so they attach together making 1 strip of 3 colors. With rolling pin, roll strip directly on cookie sheet until it measures 12×3 inches. With straight edge of knife, score strip crosswise at 1-inch intervals. Repeat with remaining ropes to make a total of 4 tri-colored strips of dough. Bake 12 to 13 minutes or until set but not completely browned; remove from oven. While cookies are still warm, trim lengthwise edges to make them even and cut into individual cookies along score marks. (Cookies will bake together but are easy to cut apart while still warm.) Cool on cookie sheets. *makes 4 dozen cookies*

Honey Almond Biscotti

½ cup butter or margarine, softened
¾ cup honey
2 eggs
1 teaspoon vanilla
3½ cups all-purpose flour
2 teaspoons ground cinnamon
2 teaspoons anise seeds
½ teaspoon salt
½ teaspoon baking powder
¼ teaspoon baking soda
1 cup dried cranberries or candied cherries
¾ cup slivered almonds

Cream butter in large bowl with electric mixer; beat in honey, eggs and vanilla. Combine flour, cinnamon, anise seeds, salt, baking powder and baking soda in small bowl; mix well. Stir into butter mixture. Stir in cranberries and nuts. Shape dough into two 10×3×1-inch logs on greased baking sheet. Bake in preheated 350°F oven about 20 minutes or until lightly browned. Remove from oven; cool 5 minutes. Remove to cutting board. *Reduce oven temperature to 300°F.* Cut each log into ½-inch strips; place on baking sheet. Bake about 20 minutes more or until crisp throughout. Cool completely on wire racks.   *makes 3 dozen cookies*

Favorite recipe from **National Honey Board**

Tip

A traditional Italian cookie, biscotti (plural of biscotto) is baked twice to produces the characteristic crunchy texture that is ideal for dipping in coffee or a dessert wine. Biscotti can be flavored with anise seed, hazelnuts, almonds or chocolate.

ACKNOWLEDGMENTS

The publisher would like to thank the companies and organizations listed below for the use of their recipes and photographs in this publication.

A.1.® Steak Sauce
American Italian Pasta Company—Pasta LaBella
Bays English Muffin Corporation
BelGioioso® Cheese, Inc.
Bestfoods
Birds Eye®
Blue Diamond Growers®
Bob Evans®
Butterball® Turkey Company
California Poultry Federation
Campbell Soup Company
ConAgra Grocery Products Company
Cucina Classica Italiana, Inc.
DAVIS® Baking Powder
Del Monte Corporation
Duncan Hines® and Moist Deluxe® are registered trademarks of Aurora Foods Inc.
Filippo Berio® Olive Oil
Fleischmann's® Original Spread

Fleischmann's® Yeast
Grey Poupon® Dijon Mustard
Hershey Foods Corporation
The HV Company
The Kingsford Products Company
Kraft Foods Holdings
Lawry's® Foods, Inc.
Lipton®
Mrs. Dash®
National Chicken Council
National Honey Board
National Pork Producers Council
Nestlé USA, Inc.
Perdue Farms Incorporated
The Procter & Gamble Company
Reckitt Benckiser
Riviana Foods Inc.
Sargento® Foods Inc.
StarKist® Seafood Company
USA Rice Federation
Wisconsin Milk Marketing Board

INDEX

Index

Index

Index

Index

Index

Index

Index

Index

Index

Index

Metric Conversion Chart

VOLUME MEASUREMENTS (dry)

$^1/_8$ teaspoon = 0.5 mL
$^1/_4$ teaspoon = 1 mL
$^1/_2$ teaspoon = 2 mL
$^3/_4$ teaspoon = 4 mL
1 teaspoon = 5 mL
1 tablespoon = 15 mL
2 tablespoons = 30 mL
$^1/_4$ cup = 60 mL
$^1/_3$ cup = 75 mL
$^1/_2$ cup = 125 mL
$^2/_3$ cup = 150 mL
$^3/_4$ cup = 175 mL
1 cup = 250 mL
2 cups = 1 pint = 500 mL
3 cups = 750 mL
4 cups = 1 quart = 1 L

VOLUME MEASUREMENTS (fluid)

1 fluid ounce (2 tablespoons) = 30 mL
4 fluid ounces ($^1/_2$ cup) = 125 mL
8 fluid ounces (1 cup) = 250 mL
12 fluid ounces (1$^1/_2$ cups) = 375 mL
16 fluid ounces (2 cups) = 500 mL

WEIGHTS (mass)

$^1/_2$ ounce = 15 g
1 ounce = 30 g
3 ounces = 90 g
4 ounces = 120 g
8 ounces = 225 g
10 ounces = 285 g
12 ounces = 360 g
16 ounces = 1 pound = 450 g

DIMENSIONS

$^1/_{16}$ inch = 2 mm
$^1/_8$ inch = 3 mm
$^1/_4$ inch = 6 mm
$^1/_2$ inch = 1.5 cm
$^3/_4$ inch = 2 cm
1 inch = 2.5 cm

OVEN TEMPERATURES

250°F = 120°C
275°F = 140°C
300°F = 150°C
325°F = 160°C
350°F = 180°C
375°F = 190°C
400°F = 200°C
425°F = 220°C
450°F = 230°C

BAKING PAN SIZES

Utensil	Size in Inches/Quarts	Metric Volume	Size in Centimeters
Baking or Cake Pan (square or rectangular)	8×8×2	2 L	20×20×5
	9×9×2	2.5 L	23×23×5
	12×8×2	3 L	30×20×5
	13×9×2	3.5 L	33×23×5
Loaf Pan	8×4×3	1.5 L	20×10×7
	9×5×3	2 L	23×13×7
Round Layer Cake Pan	8×1½	1.2 L	20×4
	9×1½	1.5 L	23×4
Pie Plate	8×1¼	750 mL	20×3
	9×1¼	1 L	23×3
Baking Dish or Casserole	1 quart	1 L	—
	1½ quart	1.5 L	—
	2 quart	2 L	—